# MADE IN THE USA

# MADE
## IN THE
# USA

## The Complete Guide to America's Finest Products

## 1992 Edition

## Made in the USA Foundation

National
Press
Books

Washington, D.C.

**Library of Congress Cataloging-in-Publication Data**

Made in the USA:
The complete guide to America's finest products
by the Made in the USA Foundation
336 pp., 15 cm. x 23 cm.
Includes index.
ISBN 0-915765-96-9; $12.95
1. Consumer eduction—United States.
2. Commercial products—United States—Catalogs.
I. Made in the USA Foundation
TX336.M33
381'.45'000973—dc20
CIP

PRINTED IN THE UNITED STATES OF AMERICA
1992 Edition

 264-C

# Acknowledgments

Many thanks to everyone at the Made in the U.S.A. Foundation, both past and present, who made this book possible. The Foundation is grateful to Ayfir Jafri, Jeff Blaydes and Eddie Meng for helping to pioneer the earliest editions of Made in the U.S.A.

Special thanks to editor Melissa Haley for shepherding this latest edition through months of research and writing and to chairman Joel D. Joseph, whose ever vigilant eyes and ears led to the discovery of countless quality American-made products.

Thanks to Alan Sultan of National Press Books for his constant advice and sense of humor and Eleanor Gorman, also of National Press, for her excellent support. Special thanks to Talia Greenberg, Jake Jakubs, Michelle Stafford and Sarah Yerkovich for assisting in the final hours of research.

We are indebted to Rick Ratliff for lending the Foundation his expertise in the car and truck chapter and to wine and beer connoisseur Ben Giliberti and toy expert Debbie Wager for their contributions.

Although it is impossible to mention everyone individually, we would like to thank the countless people in the public relations, marketing, advertising and executive offices of the companies found in this book who provided us with the necessary information to write about them. Their honesty and patience was much appreciated.

We would also like to thank the numerous trade associations and organizations that provided our researchers with advice and information, including the Crafted With Pride Council, the Bicycle Institute of America, Interbike, Footwear Industries of America and the Electronic Industries Association. Thanks also to the expert sales staffs of many local retail stores that were willing to take the time to give us their opinions on various products and manufacturers.

Finally, we would like to thank Vicki Shannon for editing the final copy of this project and all of the Americans who have inspired our continued efforts to put out the best "buy American" guide possible and who have waited so patiently for this '92 edition.

This book is dedicated to the American worker who produces the finest products in the world.

> "I have come to a resolution myself, as I hope every good citizen will, never again to purchase any article of foreign manufacture which can be had of American make, be the difference of price what it may."
>
> —Thomas Jefferson

# Contents

# Preface

Dear Concerned Citizen:

The **Made in the USA Foundation (MUSA)** is a nonprofit, educational organization that was founded in 1989 to achieve fundamental change in U.S. government policies and American consumer purchasing habits that have caused a steep decline in our nation's economic health. A trade policy of international appeasement and a lack of consumer awareness concerning the quality, availability and affordability of made in the U.S.A. products have harmed the profitability and stability of many U.S. companies resulting in the loss of millions of jobs. Our quality of life has been badly damaged.

What does "made in the USA" mean? Loose or non-existent definitions have led to a hollowing of American companies, where well-intentioned consumers are unable to distinguish high-American-content "made in the U.S.A." products from high-foreign-content, American-labeled goods.

MUSA is pursuing a dual strategy to bring about change. As a policy institute, we support and are researching legislative initiatives that would federally mandate strict content and assembly disclosure requirements; revise a tax code that now allows foreign firms to deceptively hide billions of dollars in profits from federal taxation; and enact reciprocal trade measures to ensure an open international trading arena in which U.S. companies can compete fairly. Without these fundamental changes, our stagnant economy will continue to nosedive, more and more Americans will be forced out of work, thousands more American families will suffer and we will fall further and further behind our foreign competitors. As a consumer awareness foundation, we are committed to significantly increasing consumer understanding of the critical importance of purchasing products made in the U.S.A. By purchasing goods made in the U.S.A., the American consumer will help revitalize our economy, put millions of Americans back to work and improve the quality of life for all of us. We provide consumers with accurate information to allow them to differentiate high-American-content, U.S.-made goods from American shell or foreign goods. This annual publication, *Made in the USA: The Complete Guide to America's Finest Products*, is just one resource we provide consumers to make it easier to buy American. As our organization expands, we wish to establish additional consumer resources, including a consumer hot line to offer up-to-date information on American goods.

We believe that the policy proposals we offer and the consumer services we provide are absolutely critical to our nation's economic well-being. If we do not put America back to work by using our consumer dollars to purchase goods made in the U.S.A., millions more jobs will be lost and we will soon become an economic weakling.

Foreign countries are buying our land and our businesses; individual American taxpayers pay a higher rate of taxation than billion-dollar foreign corporations doing business here; big-name U.S. officials race through the revolving door into the waiting arms of wealthy foreign corporations that pay them outrageous sums to peddle influence in Washington; and through it all the American worker suffers. **THE TIME FOR FUNDAMENTAL CHANGE IS NOW!** Why should three of every five foreign firms pay **NO FEDERAL INCOME TAX** on hundreds of billions of dollars of sales? Why should we allow foreign competitors open access to our marketplace when they won't allow us the same courtesy? And why can't it be simple to easily identify high quality, highly affordable made in the U.S.A. goods?

The Made in the USA Foundation will not rest until critically needed changes are made, American workers are back at work and the U.S. has regained the mantle of economic leadership in the international arena.

If you want to make a better America for ourselves and for our children, then please join us in this battle. Inside this book you will find information about how to join with the

Made in the USA Foundation to bring about badly needed change. (If the pull-out application for joining the Foundation is missing, or you would like an extra copy for a friend, contact us and we will send you another application form.) I look forward to hearing from you soon. Our nation's well-being is at stake!

Sincerely,

Brian T. Flood
Executive Director, MUSA

---

**MADE IN THE USA FOUNDATION**

1800 Diagonal Rd.
Suite 180
Alexandria, VA  22314

(800) ASK-MUSA General Information
(703) 519-6100      Offices

---

# Introduction

Welcome to the 1992 edition of **Made in the U.S.A.: The Complete Guide to America's Finest Products.** This third edition is the Foundation's latest effort toward publishing the ultimate guidebook for consumers who want to buy quality American-made products.

## Why This Guide

The Made in the U.S.A. Foundation publishes this buyer's guide to quality American-made products for several reasons. First, we want to assist those consumers who already want to buy American but find doing so difficult and confusing. In these tough economic times, the demand for this book is particularly strong.

Second, the Foundation would like to change the popular notion that "nothing" is made in the U.S. anymore and that what is made here is inferior in quality. This is an incorrect impression that we believe a quick flip through the following pages will dispel.

Along the same lines, the Foundation wants to show the world the splendid array of quality American-made products. We are quite proud of the fact that our publisher has arranged to have this book translated into Japanese.

Perhaps most importantly, the Foundation is deeply committed to educating consumers about the philosophy of "buying American." We hope to encourage enough consumers to buy quality American-made products that there will be a positive effect on our troubled economy and our chronic trade deficit. American manufacturers could use a boost, and we hope this book is part of a widespread "buy American" movement that gives it to them. Although our economic malaise and manufacturing decline are complex problems with many sides and without a clear, singular solution, buying American-made products is one way the consumer can aid our national economy.

# Why Buy American

As noted above, one compelling reason to buy American is that it is a direct way to help our struggling economy and the besieged American manufacturing sector. It is a way to keep jobs and money in the United States—two things our country desperately requires for economic recovery.

Another good reason to buy American is that it is usually in your best interest as a consumer to do so. The Foundation believes most of the time the best American products are the best products in the world of their type. American products tend to be safer and, although often more expensive initially, they embody a better long-run value. They are designed for American standards and uses, and it is easy to find replacement parts. Finally, American products embody a cherished way of life.

# Buying Into A Way of Life

When you purchase an American-made product, you are also paying for the American way of life. American products may be more expensive for very good reasons. Their prices include the costs of:

1. *Consumer protection*
2. *Environmental protection*
3. *Safe, humane working conditions*
4. *Decent worker wages*

In contrast, products from other countries are cheaper because the nations they come from do not have the high standard of living that we value in this country. Many of them employ practices and wages that the United States ended centuries ago. For instance, imported goods may well be produced by child or prison labor or in factory or workroom conditions that would never be acceptable in the United States. Many do not have minimum wage requirements or worker protection laws. The prison labor and appalling conditions of Chinese factories have been well-documented. So have the environmental degradation, child labor and exploitative wages in the Mexican maquilladora factories.

All things considered, when you buy a quality American-made product, you are purchasing a piece of a society with the most freedom and highest standard of living of any nation in the entire world. To help retain this way of life we all enjoy, we must continually invest in it, and buying American is one very important way to do so.

# But Should I Buy American At All Costs?

The Foundation does not recommend that you purchase poorly made American products. If the free marketplace, which is the cornerstone of capitalism, is to work, consumers must search for and purchase the highest quality products possible. However, there are quality American-made products in virtually every consumer category. With the help of this book, we hope that you will find and purchase American products every time.

# Made in the U.S.A. 1992

This year, we have added many new companies and products. We are pleased to include Buell Motor Co.—a new U.S. sport motorcycle manufacturer—and Cooper Tire. We have significantly expanded the chapters covering some of consumers' most frequent purchases—clothing, footwear and toys and games—to include such companies as Rocky Boots of Nelson, Ohio, Danner Boots of Portland, Ore., Intempo Toys of Palo Alto, Calif., and Pendleton Woolen Mills of Portland.

Unfortunately, we have also had to remove a few listings. Keystone cameras, which had been the country's sole remaining manufacturer of 35mm cameras, this year filed for bankruptcy protection, was bought and promptly moved production overseas. As of March, the U.S. also loses its last American-owned domestic television manufacturer as Zenith moves its last whole-set assembly operation from Springfield, Mo. to Mexico.

Keeping track of the quality products made in the U.S.A. is a tremendous task. The number of products on the market is practically infinite and production is constantly shifting. Consequently, producing this shopping guide is an ongoing process. We are confident that the buy-American shopper will find this book an excellent aid in purchasing everything from a ball point pen to a new car or truck. We also know the reader will invariably want even more information—more companies, more consumer categories, more detailed content information, etc. To these readers we must say we are getting there—please bear with us as we continue to enlarge and develop our buy-American guide.

All of that aside, the book you now hold in your hands is the most comprehensive, interesting and readable catalogue of America's finest products. From stuffed animals to grand pianos, this book will point you in the right direction. Whenever possible, we tell you name brands, company history and ownership, exactly where the product is made, how to find it, price range and a company phone number. Each chapter also attempts to give you a general idea of the health of that particular industry. We will continue to expand and standardize this type of information with each coming year.

# The Definition of American-Made

Ideally, each of the products found in this book would be manufactured by American-owned companies and contain 100% American-made component parts. However, in today's global marketplace, such products rarely exist.

All of the products recommended in this publication are manufactured or assembled in the United States. Most of them contain some imported parts, although the vast majority contain at least majority U.S. content (51% and above). When there was no alternative, or we felt it was a topic we must address—as with automobiles—we note products manufactured by foreign companies in the U.S. In rare cases, we note products that are merely assembled in the U.S. and probably contain a high percentage of imported components. However, rest assured that in every case we list the best, most "all-American" products we could find.

# Checklist For Shopping American

This book will give you a head start in "shopping American." However, when venturing into categories this guide does not cover, or when doing any purchasing at all, keep the following simple rules of thumb in mind:

**1. Read labels**

Look for products clearly labelled "Made in the U.S.A."

Don't be shy. Open the box or turn the item over, but find the phrase that states where it was made. This is the only way to make absolutely sure a product is or is not made in the United States.

## 2. Don't Assume Anything

Don't assume a product sold by an American company or advertised or marked with "American," the American flag or other patriotic symbols is actually made in the U.S. Many such items are not.

Don't assume salespeople, or even the customer service departments of companies, know where a product is made. Oftentimes they do not. Ask plenty of questions and whenever possible examine the item yourself.

## 3. When in doubt, see #1

Remember, the label "Made in the U.S.A." is your only true guarantee that a product is made in the United States.

"Designed in the U.S.," "Engineered in the U.S." and other such phrases are usually smoke screens for imported goods.

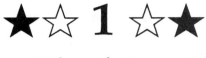

# Clothing

## The Industry

According to the Crafted With Pride Council, the U.S. fiber, textile and apparel sector employs 2.1 million Americans—one out of 11 U.S. manufacturing jobs. This is more than the petroleum refining, primary metals or aircraft industries and two and a half times the number of Americans employed in the automotive industry.

However, since 1980, approximately 581,480 jobs have been lost in the fiber, textile and apparel industry. Indeed, in 1990 alone, approximately 95,500 U.S. jobs were lost in this field. Although the U.S. textile and apparel industry used to be one of the nation's leading earners of foreign exchange, in 1990 it accounted for one-quarter of our nation's multi-billion dollar trade deficit. Most telling of all is the fact that in the last decade, textile and apparel imports into the U.S. have tripled—most of them coming from nations with unjust working conditions, including, in the case of China, forced labor.

Clearly, the textile and apparel industry is under siege. By making a commitment to purchase American-made clothing—preferably crafted from U.S. materials—consumers can help stop this alarming loss of jobs and national revenue.

## American-Made Clothing

Looking for American-made clothing can be a chore. Oftentimes, it seems as though there is very little American clothing available. Turning over tags in stores and scouring advertisements for an indication of where a piece of clothing was made is a tedious and often frustrating process. This section provides general shopping tips and a list of American-made brand names that should make your shopping much easier. For the moment, however, let's discuss why you should look for American-made clothing in the first place.

Aside from helping ease the decimation of the American apparel and fabric industry, shopping for American clothing makes good sense. For one thing, American-made clothing is typically of much higher quality than imported clothing. American clothing is usually made from better materials, and sewn more carefully than its imported counterparts (excluding top-of-the-line designer clothing and specialty items such as Irish hand-knit sweaters).

Although the high quality of American clothing often makes it more expensive, it is worth the price in terms of durability. Ask yourself how many cheap imported bargain clothes you have thrown out after just one season because they shrank, ripped or showed undue wear.

American-made clothing also tends to be of a classic or non-faddish style that makes it a good wardrobe investment. Cheap, here-one-season-gone-the-next imported fad clothing must constantly be replaced, whereas a high quality, classic piece of American clothing will be around for years to come.

Finally, American-made clothing is designed for the American body build and consequently fits better than a lot of imported clothing.

# Read Your Labels

The easiest way to find American-made clothing when you are shopping is to read labels. Federal law requires every piece of clothing sold in the United States to carry a tag that tells the consumer where the garment was manufactured and where the component materials originated. This labeling requirement makes it far easier to determine exactly what you are getting when you purchase a piece of clothing than with other consumer products. For instance, a piece of clothing made in the U.S. from U.S. fabrics will have a label that simply says, "Made in the U.S.A." Clothing manufactured in the U.S. from imported fabric will read, "Made in the U.S.A. of imported fabric(s)," "Made in the U.S.A., fabric from Germany, India, etc.," or something similar. Clothing made here from both domestic and imported fabrics will say just that. Finally, imported clothing will say, "Made in Indonesia, Malaysia," or whatever country the clothing came from.

Finding the label that states this manufacturing information is usually easy. Although it occasionally appears on the hang tags, the best place to look is on the clothing itself— most often at the top of the inside of the garment. If you have trouble finding the tag, turn the garment inside out and check all the seams for the manufacturing information tag. Only on rare occasion will you find a completely unmarked garment. If the salesperson cannot help you locate a tag, assume the garment is imported. (American clothing manufacturers are eager to mark their products "Made in the U.S.A.")

Never assume that clothing is actually made in the U.S. just because it is branded with a name that includes the word "American," is advertised or otherwise marked as being "American," or uses such phrases as "an American classic" or "an American tradition." Many companies import clothing, call it American this or that and hope consumers will assume it is American-made.

By the same token, don't assume a foreign sounding name is manufactured abroad. Not only do many American companies have names that reflect the "old country," but many foreign companies do some of their manufacturing here.

Finally, clothing sold under historically American-made name brands does not ensure that it is made in the U.S. As with many industries, many U.S. clothing companies now mix production between domestic and offshore or they strictly import.

# Recommended Stores

With the exception of shops like *Pier 1* that set out to sell only imported goods, almost every store that sells clothing will have some that is American-made. The challenge is reading labels and finding out exactly what is what. However, some stores carry a larger selection of American-made clothing than others. Find those stores and patronize them.

Here are a few of the stores that the Foundation staff has found to carry a good selection of American-made clothing:

**Brooks Brothers**
**The Gap** *(50% U.S. made)*
**Kmart**
**Kuppenheimer** *(men's)*
**J.C. Penney**
**Richmond Brothers** *(men's)*
**Sears**
**Hart Schaffner and Marx Stores**
*(men's;* including Wallachs, Raleighs, Baskin, Silverwoods, Hastings, Jas. K. Wilson, Zachry, Leopold, Price & Rolle, Anton's, Wolf Brothers, Klopfenstein's, Walker's, Porter-Stevens, Hanny's, Liemandt's, Field Bros., Peer Gordon and Kleinhans).

# Recommended Brand Names

In any store, it helps to know brand names that make all or a good amount of their clothing in the U.S. This saves a great deal of time and frustration turning over labels. What follows is a brand by brand, company by company look at some of the best American clothing manufacturers. Although it is far from comprehensive, it should give the consumer a healthy start when looking for American-made clothing.

# Suits and Sport Coats

### Brooks Brothers *(Men's and Women's )*

**Brooks Brothers** manufactures around 90% of its moderately priced yet high quality men's and women's suits and blazers in the U.S. Brooks Brothers suits fall in the $300-$600 range, although the company offers custom-tailored suits that may go as high as $1,000.

*Brooks Brothers men's blazer and women's suit*

Traditional blazers range from $175-$375. Brooks Brothers suits and blazers can be purchased in Brooks Brothers' own stores or by catalogue.

☎ *(800) 274-1815  (Brooks Brothers)*

## Kuppenheimer *(Men's)*

**Kuppenheimer** sells inexpensive, good quality suits and sport jackets in Kuppenheimer stores across the country. An average Kuppenheimer suit costs around $175; a sport coat $100. Although Kuppenheimer still makes all of its suit coats, sportcoats and slacks in the U.S., Kuppenheimer accessories, particularly topcoats, are increasingly imported.

☎ *(800) 447-6751 (Kuppenheimer)*

## Oxxford *(Men's)*

**Oxxford Clothes** makes what are widely considered the best American-made tailored suits and sport jackets. Oxxford suits and sport coats have been almost entirely hand-made in the company's Chicago work rooms for over 75 years. The quality of Oxxford is so well-known that the company does not do any advertising but instead relies on word-of-mouth.

Oxxford suits retail for $1,000 and up, with Oxxford sport coats in the $800 range. Oxxford recently expanded its products to include finely crafted shirts ($100) and ties ($60-$75). Oxxford clothing can be found at Bergdorf Goodman, Tripler's, Saks Fifth Avenue, Barneys New York and other fine clothing and department stores.

## Pendleton *(Women's )*

**Pendleton Woolen Mills** of Portland, Ore., manufactures excellent women's suits available in better department and clothing stores nationwide under **Sophisticates of Pendleton** and **The Pendleton Collection**. All Pendleton suits are manufactured in Portland. These suits are worth every stitch of their rather expensive price tags. For more information, see the Pendleton listing in the Casual section of this chapter.

☎ *(503) 226-4801 (Pendleton)*

*"Miss Pendleton" suit*

## Richmond Brothers *(Men's)*

**Richmond Brothers** offers moderately priced, American-made suits and sport coats in Richmond Brothers stores and dealers nationwide.

### Other suits *(Men's)*

Some other moderately priced, U.S.-made suits can be found under the *Atwood, Joseph Abood, Haspel, Halston, Hart Schaffner & Marx, Hickey-Freeman, Palm Beach* and *Pferris* brand names.

### Other Suits *(Women's)*

The following designers make quality women's suits in the U.S. Many of them also import some of their suits. So look for these name brands, and then check your labels: *Ralph Lauren, Jones N.Y., Evan Picone, Shelli Segal, Paul Stanley, Bert Newman, Christian Dior, Noviello-Bloom, Georges Marciano, Saville, E.R. Girard, Nicole Miller, Albert Nipon, PSI Couture, Morgan Miller* and *Gianni Sport.*

# Designer Clothing

*A Word on Designers...*

Designers make their clothing all over the world. Clothing bearing a European designer's name does not necessarily mean that clothing is imported. For example, many men's European designers manufacture clothing, particularly suits and sport jackets, in the U.S., including Austin-Reed, Burberry's, Ungaro of Paris and Christian Dior. So, if you are a designer shopper and want to shop American, don't discount European names: check your labels—you may be surprised at what you find.

By the same token, some American designers do very little production in the U.S. For example, Liz Claiborne makes next to nothing here. In addition, although Perry Ellis makes its tailored clothing in the U.S., it also does a significant amount of importing. Ellis' "American Series," men's clothing line and women's "America Casual Wear"— which are almost entirely imported save a few logo cotton T-shirts—are particularly disappointing.

All of the designer clothing mentioned below offers all or largely U.S.-made clothing. This clothing can be found at better department and specialty clothing stores nationwide.

## <u>Designer Coats</u> *(Women's)*

Interestingly enough, many designers—even those that do very little manufacturing in the U.S.—make top-quality coats in the U.S. Designers that manufacture women's coats here include *Anne Klein, Perry Ellis, Christian Dior, Calvin Klein, Evan-Picone, Fashions by Jill, Karen, Tahari, Bicci, Jones New York, J.G. Hook, Liz Callahan* and *Carole Cohen.*

## *Recommended Designers*

### Henry Grethel  *(Men's)*

**Henry Grethel** is an American designer that strives to produce an "international" men's clothing line, yet it does a great deal of manufacturing in the U.S.

### Georges Marciano  *(Women's)*

The **Georges Marciano Boutique Collection** is designer Georges Marciano's signature collection of sophisticated career and lifestyle wear that encourages women to think in terms of wardrobe building. This premier mix of jackets, skirts, pants and shorts is available in an abundance of bold and subtle

*Georges Marciano double-breasted jacket and Hollywood waist pant*

27

colors, patterns and styles in top quality materials, including wool and silk. Georges Marciano prides himself on manufacturing the majority of his clothing in the U.S.

Marciano also designs a full line of American-made **Guess?** casual clothing which is discussed in the next section.

### Carole Miller *(Women's)*

Carole Miller makes a good selection of women's dress clothing in the U.S., including a variety of very attractive skirt and blouse sets.

### Albert Nipon *(Women's)*

Albert Nipon manufactures many of its top-of-the-line women's designer dress fashions in the U.S.

# Men's Dress Shirts

It is fairly easy to find quality men's dress shirts made in the U.S.A. Most department stores offer American-made shirts under their own label. *Eagle, Hathaway, Christian Dior* and *Burberry* make dress shirts in the U.S., as do countless other companies.

# Women's Blouses

It is also relatively easy to find high quality women's blouses made in the U.S.A. *Evan Picone, Carole Little, Shelli Segal, Finity, Gianni Sport, Georges Marciano, J.C. Penney's Worthington, Sag Harbor, Calvin Klein* and *Brooks Brothers* are some of the name brand women's blouses that are often made in the U.S.

# Casual Clothing

### Alps Sportswear *(Sweaters)*

**Alps Sportswear** was founded as a family business in Boston, Mass., in 1934. Alps offers a large variety of comfortable, well-sized, traditionally styled natural fiber sweaters that are suitable for all sorts of leisure and outdoor activity.

These sweaters are available in men's and women's, full and vest, button up and pull-over, crew neck and high neck styles in 100% cotton, 100% virgin worsted wool and wool blends.

Alps sweaters are moderately priced at approximately $20-$35.

Alps also offers high quality cotton turtlenecks, shorts and T-shirts as well as "Moose Fleece" pullovers and 100% cotton afghans.

*Alps sweaters*

All Alps products are made in Berwick, PA and are available in clothing and outdoor shops nationwide.

☎ *(508) 683-2438 (Alps Sportswear)*

### Cooper Sportswear

Cooper Sportwear was the original supplier of A-2 leather flight jackets to the U.S. Air Force during WWII. More than 45 years later, these jackets are again official clothing for the Air Force. These top-quality, American-made jackets are currently manufactured by **MBI Flight Gear** and may be individually ordered by calling MBI. Each jacket costs $206, including shipping.

☎ *(800) 367-4534 (Cooper)*

## Cross Creek *(Knit Shirts)*

**Cross Creek Apparel** has been making all of its high quality leisure clothing in the U.S. since 1935. In fact, the company's dealer catalogue boasts, "As always, the Cross Creek Collection is made proudly and completely in the United States." Cross Creek is best known for its excellent men's knit shirts. All Cross Creek knits are short-sleeved shirts sporting solids and stripes, collared and jersey styles in cotton pique or combed cotton. Cross Creek also offers a men's turtleneck or two and a **Pro Collection** golf line that features several women's knit shirts, Cross Creek logo knit tops and men's shorts and pants. Cross Creek tops are well-made, durable shirts that are well worth their price tag. Cross Creek shirts and other products are available at better department stores nationwide.

☎ *(800) 877-8361 (Cross Creek )*

*A Cross Creek Pro Collection knit golf shirt and cotton jersey*

## Crossings *(Sweaters and Knits)*

**Crossings** is a subsidiary of **Geneco Co.** Crossings makes all of its fashionable, natural fiber men's cotton and wool sweaters in Garden City, N.J. Since 1991, the company has also been making women's sweaters and a variety of men's and women's related knit separates—approximately 20% of which are imported. Crossings clothing is available at better department price and specialty stores nationwide.

☎ *(800) 544-6279 (Crossings)*

*Textured crew-neck sweater from Crossings*

## Hue *(Women's Tights and Leggings)*

**Hue,** a division of **Moskal and Chilewich**, is quite an American entrepreneurial success story. In 1978, business partners Kathy Moskal and Sandy Chilewich revolutionized the women's legwear industry by introducing an array of bright colorful cotton tights. The company has grown by leaps and bounds, creating and then dominating U.S.

fashion trends, and working its way to the top of the casual legwear industry.

Hue manufactures a stunning variety of colored, patterned, lace and other innovative tights, leggings and shorts, as well as unique bodywear. The company recently introduced maternity, large sizes and little girl's legwear. All of Hue's 54 styles and 25 colors are manufactured in Mebane, N.C., and can be found in better department and specialty stores nationwide.

*Hue gingham cuff leggings and polka dot cuff leggings*

## Guess? *(Jeans and Casual Clothing)*

In 1981, Georges Marciano was already a successful designer, manufacturer and retailer when he first introduced a line of all American-made, first-ever stone-washed **Guess?** jeans. The jeans were an overwhelming smash and Marciano went on to develop an entire line of casual Guess? clothing.

Guess? clothing for men and women includes Marciano's award-winning jeans, as well as comfortable, highly durable skirts and jackets—all designed to "shake up the imagination" and convey that certain Guess? mystique. Although denim figures prominently in Guess? clothing, it also includes crepe, gabardine, rayon, organza, and silk. Marciano's men's collection runs the gamut from rugged wear to dressier separates, including jeans, jackets, blazers, knitwear and a variety of prints—all featuring the traditional flair of the Wild West. Guess? also makes children's and infant clothing, which is discussed in the Children's Clothing section of this chapter.

*5-pocket Guess? jeans with denim and blanket jackets (l) and Guess? rugged denim Western shirt and wide wale corduroys (r)*

Although originally from France, Marciano now resides in California and takes particular pride in the fact that approximately 90% of Guess? clothing and all Guess? jeans are manufactured in the United States. Guess? clothing can be found in better department and clothing stores nationwide.

## OshKosh *(Men's and Women's)*

OshKosh women's overalls

**OshKosh B'Gosh**'s hickory striped denim bib overalls were first worn in the late 1800s by frontier workers and farmers whose jobs required sturdy rugged clothing. Today, OshKosh B'Gosh still offers a line of basic, rugged workwear, but primarily produces casual bib overalls for adults and children. The majority of Osh Kosh clothing is still made in the United States.

## Ruff Hewn *(Men's and Women's )*

**Ruff Hewn** clothing for men and women is manufactured by **W & J Rives**. The clothing is named for Barclay Ruffin Hewn ("Ruff"), an American adventurer who pitched in to help outfit the 1900 U.S. Olympics team and who made the Utility Work Clothing for the New Deal's National Industrial Recovery Act and the uniforms of the WWI Allied forces.

Ruff Hewn clothing is practical, classically styled, quality clothing that is designed for a wide range of after-work activities. From jeans, khakis and casual skirts to blazers and dress shirts/blouses, Ruff Hewn clothing is meant to capture comfort and an individualistic style—while evoking a mood that recalls American heroes and the American spirit of adventure. Ruff Hewn clothing is approximately 90% made in the U.S. and is sold in major department stores nationwide.

*(800) 334-8716 (Ruff Hewn)*

*Ruff Hewn men's and women's casual outfits*

## Pendleton

**Pendleton Woolen Mills** of Portland, Ore., has been known for high quality woolen goods since 1895, when it produced robes for the Indian trade and bed blankets and finished woolen goods for Western settlers. A family-owned business, Pendleton is a completely vertically integrated company that performs every step in processing—from raw wool to the finished product—here in the U.S. This makes Pendleton clothing about as American as you can get. As the company explains, "At Pendleton, we control the entire manufacturing process ourselves. Under our own roofs, here in America."

Pendleton's Oregon, Washinton, Nebraska and Iowa plants manufacture top-quality 100% wool men's and women's dress and casual clothing, including the extraordinary men's Pendleton shirt, which is available in five different weights, 12 different styles and over 100 exclusive fabric designs.

*Timberland brush plaid jacket and snap front Western shirt by Pendleton*

*Knockabout jacket and shorts by Pendleton*

Pendleton men's sportswear includes outerwear, pants, sport coats, sweaters and robes, which are sold in five Pendleton lines: **Pendleton, Country Traditions, High Grade Western Wear, Big & Tall** and **Lobo.**

Women's dress-casual styles are sold under the **Knock-abouts** line. The company also continues to manufacture Indian blankets.

Pendleton clothing is fairly expensive. However, timely yet timeless design, 100% virgin wool and vertical manufacturing make Pendleton clothing an unbeatable buy for its American-made quality and value.

## Queensboro Shirt Co.

**Queensboro Shirt Co.** specializes in custom embroidered, American-made 100% cotton logo polo and golf shirts. Queensboro also offers logo sweatshirts, sweaters, baseball hats and tote bags. The company is dedicated to offering superior quality, beautifully embroidered clothing, quickly, courteously and at a reasonable cost. Queensboro believes so strongly that its products are some of the absolute best that it guarantees every one of them and vows, "At any time, for any reason, you have the right to return anything you buy from us for a full refund or replacement."

Queensboro shirts are available in both long and short sleeve for approximately $20-$37 each, depending on the quantity bought. Queensboro's other items range from approximately $20 a tote bag to $32 a sweater—also depending on the number ordered.

The company will work from an existing logo or help you create a new one. All Queensboro products are manufactured in the U.S. in Tennessee, New Jersey or North Carolina, and are ideal for groups or businesses that want promotional or employee logo products to be American-made.

☎ *(800) 274-4787 (Queensboro Shirt Co.)*

# Jeans

Despite the United States' reputation as the world's source of blue jeans, jeans sold in the U.S. are a mix of imported and domestic pairs. To varying degrees, all of the big name brand jeans are still manufactured in the states. To help you with your label watching, here is the breakdown for major name brand jeans sold in the U.S.A.:

**Calvin Klein**—*100% made in the U.S.A.*
**Guess?**—*100% made in the U.S.A.*
**Wrangler** —*100% made in the U.S.A.*
**Levi**—*approximately 95% made in the U.S.A.*
**Jordach**e—*"most" made in the U.S.A.*
**Lee** —*"some" made in the U.S.A.*
**Gap**—*men's 90% made in the U.S; women's 50%*
**Weekends** *(J.C. Penney)—some made in the U.S.A.*
**Rustler**—*imported.*

# Children's Clothing

The following companies manufacture children's clothing in the U.S.:

## Infants and Toddlers

**Carters**
**Healthtex**
**Baby Guess?**
**Land's End Catalogue**
**OshKosh**

## Children's Clothing

### Heavy U.S. Production

**Body Glove**—*Girls' actionwear.*
**Brooks Brothers**—*Boys' dress-casual clothing; 90% U.S.-made.*
            ☎ *(800) 274-1815*
**Bull Frog**—*Jogsuits and 2-piece fleece outfits; over 80% U.S.-made.*
**Crayola Kids**—*Bright colorful boys' and girls' clothes; all U.S.-made; available through Spiegel catalogue.*

☎ *(800) 345-5000*

**Guess? Kids**—*Boys' and girls' trend-setting apparel; 90% made in the U.S.A.*

**Hue**—*Girls' tights, leggings and bodywear; all American-made.*

**OshKosh**—*Infant and children's wear, including the classic Osh-Kosh denim overalls; majority U.S. made.*

**LA Movers**—*Boys', girls' and misses sportswear; available Penney's, Sears, Ames, Target, etc.: 100% U.S. made.*

**Lands' End catalogue**—☎ *(800) 356-4444.*

**Palmetto's**—*Casual boys' and girls' wear; approximately 60-65% U.S. made.*

**Russell**—*Boys' and girls' sportswear; 100% U.S. made.*

**Zonk**—*Boys' and young men's T-shirts and beachwear; 100% made in Portland, Ore.*

*Brooks Brothers boys' hopsack blazer, bold stripe shirt and chinos*

Kids' Guess? clothing

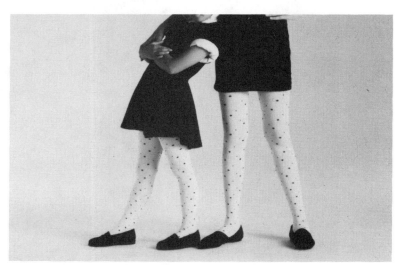

Girls' dizzy dot tights by Hue

*OshKosh toddlers' overalls and children's clothing*

## Some U.S. production

### Cherokee
**Everlast**—*Boys' and girls' active/sportswear sold under Everlast, Bum, Nautica and Riddell labels; about 50% U.S.-made.*
**Gap Kids**—*Jeans and cotton separates; approximately 50% U.S.-made.*
**Lees**—*Boys' and girls' jeans and other denim clothing; mixed production.*
**Levi**—*Denim basics, casual dress clothes for infants through youth; not as much U.S. production as you would think—check your tags.*
**Pacific Coast Highway**—*Boys' and young mens' sportswear; approximately 40% U.S.-made, although the company is trying to shift more production back to the U.S.*

**Strike Four**
**Surfers Alliance**
**TFW**—*Boys' and young men's sport and dresswear; approximately 50% made in U.S.*

# Athletic and Outdoor Clothing

## Champion Sportswear

Champion manufactures some of the highest quality athletic wear available. Champion offers a full line of athletic clothing, including heavy duty T-shirts and shorts and its well-known line of fleece sweatshirts and sweatpants. Although Champion sportswear is fairly expensive as sweats go, it is very well-made, durable sportswear that is worth the initial investment.

Approximately 90% of Champion sportswear is made in the U.S.

## Russell

Russell makes 100% of its excellent sportswear sold in the U.S. in Alabama, Georgia, North Carolina, Florida and Virginia. Russell sportswear can be purchased in department and sporting goods

*Russell athletic clothing*

stores nationwide or through the L.L. Bean catalogue.

## Everlast

**U.S.A. Classic** manufactures about half of its **Everlast Bum** (children), **Nautica** (youthwear) and **Riddell** active wear in the U.S. in Tennessee and Alabama.

## Gore-Tex®

**Gore-Tex** is a highly durable, breathable, waterproof fabric that revolutionized outdoor clothing, footwear and accessories. This unique fabric, which is found in a wide range of items all over the world, was developed in 1969 by Bob Gore as a spin-off of his Newark, Del., company's work with polytetrafluoroethylene-insulated electronic cables.

Today, **W.L. Gore and Associates** is still headquartered in Delaware, but is now a global company with plants and offices around the world. However, Gore-Tex fabric for the U.S. market is manufactured in Elkton, Md. Companies that purchase this fabric may or may not assemble the final garment in the U.S., although most do. So, although a Gore-Tex tag usually means a U.S. garment, it is really only a guarantee of American-made fabrics—so watch your labels.

That being said, the best source of **American-made rainwear** and other waterproof clothing is that constructed from Gore-Tex. It has an unsurpassed degree of durability and a combination of waterproof/breathability ideal for any type of outdoor activity. Gore-Tex waterproof outerwear is state-of-the-art clothing that, although expensive, is simply the best that money can buy and pays for itself in durability and function. Best of all, Gore-Tex rainwear sold in the U.S. is usually assembled in the U.S. This stands in stark contrast to the all-imported coated nylon and plastic rainwear that is always imported.

☎ *(800) 431-GORE (Gore and Associates)*

## Patagonia

**Patagonia**, a subsidiary of **Lost Arrow Corp.**, is a California-based firm that manufactures roughly 60% of its top-notch outdoor clothing in the United States.

Patagonia's 100% U.S.-made **Capilene® long underwear** is ideal for winter sporting activities or outdoor work situations. Patagonia Capilene® underwear is by far the best long underwear on the market. The underwear is constructed from North Carolina-made capilene, which not only insulates but "wicks" moisture away from the skin. Consequently, this capilene underwear does not get wet and clammy like cotton long underwear, but actually pulls moisture away from the body and then dries itself with the wearer's body heat. As any outdoor enthusiast knows, staying dry is half the battle in keeping warm.

Patagonia's capilene underwear is superior to other "wicking" polyester underwear, like polypropilene, in that it does not retain odor and can be machine dried. Patagonia Capilene® long underwear is available in four different weights to suit various type of activities and is available in both children's and adult sizes. Patagonia clothing can be found in outdoor and wilderness shops nationwide or ordered through the Patagonia catalogue.

☎ *(800) 638-6464 (Patagonia)*

## Wigwam *(Socks, Hats and Gloves)*

When cold weather strikes, Wigwam accessories are the place to look for relief. **Wigwam Mills** makes hundreds of socks for athletics, outdoor activities and casual wear and a large assortment of knit hats and gloves. Wigwam accessories are all manufactured in Sheboygan, Wis., and are exported everywhere, including Taiwan, Japan, Italy, France, Germany and Scandinavia. Although Wigwam accessories may be a bit more expensive than other brands, they are a deal in terms of quality. Says Senior Vice President Gene

Oeschger, "We make a quality product and everyone in the world is willing to pay a little more for it."

# Mail-Order Catalogue Shopping

Shopping by catalogue is an easy way to find American-made clothing. This is because all mail-order catalogues must mark each and every item as either "imported" or "made in the U.S." Flipping through the pages of a catalogue can be much easier than searching for labels among racks of store-bought clothing. There are two U.S. catalogue companies that offer a great deal of American-made clothing:

## L.L. Bean

It all started in 1812 when Leon Leonwood Bean started making and selling mail-order "Maine Hunting Shoes" out of his brother's Freeport, Maine, dry goods store. Although the original Maine Hunting Shoe was a disaster and 90 out of the first 100 were returned, Bean refunded or replaced every pair with an improved Maine Hunting Shoe. The rest, as they say, is history.

L.L. Bean has grown into a massive mail-order company that offers 5,500 different items in over 20 yearly catalogues, including outdoor and casual clothing, shoes, a variety of household and outdoor goods—and, of course, the Maine Hunting Shoe. Some things, however, have not changed. L.L. Bean still sells basic, quality, durable goods that carry an unconditional 100% guarantee and L.L. Bean's retail stores and phone lines are still open 24 hours a day, much in the same way that Leon Bean used to oblige needy hunters who stopped at the dry goods store in the middle of the night. Best of all, well over 90% of the goods in L.L. Bean catalogues are made in the U.S.—either by Bean's Brunswick, Maine. manufacturing facility or by other U.S. companies.

L.L. Bean products can be purchased at factory outlets in Maine and New Hampshire, the 24-hour Freeport, Maine retail store or by mail.

☎ *(800) 341-4341 (L .L. Bean-24 hrs.)*

## Lands' End

**Lands' End** began as a small manufacturer of racing sailboat equipment and rainsuits in a Chicago basement in 1963. As the company expanded into a full-fledged mail-order company that sold casual and outdoor clothing, footwear and household and outdoor goods, it moved to the tiny town of Dodgeville, Wis. Lands' End remains in Dodgeville where it takes special pride in the joy and dedication of its workers.

Although Lands' End offers a few more imported goods than L.L. Bean, "made in the U.S.A." merchandise manufactured by Lands' End's Dodgeville workers or its U.S. suppliers dominates the pages of the catalogue. One advantage of the Lands' End catalogue is that it includes a large assortment of American-made children's and infant wear. All Lands' End products are submitted to rigorous quality inspection, are guaranteed and are shipped within 36 hours (48 for monogrammed items).

☎ *(800) 356-4444 (Lands' End 24-hour)*

# Footwear

## The Industry

Despite the fact that American footwear is considered among the finest in the world, the U.S. shoe industry is in trouble. Imports rose 412% from 1968 to 1990, while domestic production dropped so low that the U.S. now produces fewer shoes per capita than during the Great Depression. This flood of imported shoes has cost Americans jobs and weakened the high standards Americans have become accustomed to in their footwear.

Some consumers buy European shoes because they think they are more stylish. European shoes (women's in particular) may appear more elegant, but many are built from shoe lasts (molds) purchased from Asian countries, where people generally have smaller and narrower feet than in the West. Consequently, many stylish pairs of European shoes are uncomfortable and even painful.

Consumers also choose imported shoes because they are generally cheaper. However, cheap imports are like cheap anything else—what you save at the register, you lose in terms of durability and quality. U.S. shoe manufacturers produce much less than their European and Asian competition. Consequently, U.S. shoe manufacturers concentrate on quality—not quantity—and continue to earn American shoes a worldwide reputation for comfort, durability and unrivaled quality.

# Athletic shoes

Although the athletic shoe market is dominated by imports and Nikes and Reeboks seem to be everywhere, there are a few manufacturers of high quality American-made athletic shoes.

## New Balance

**New Balance Athletic Shoe** began in 1906. Although the company originally produced arch supports and orthopedic shoes, in the mid-1950s New Balance began to work with runners to manufacture custom-made running shoes. In 1976, New Balance introduced the **M320** running shoe, which was named the number one shoe on the market by *Runners World* magazine. New Balance has been in the top ranks of the athletic shoe industry ever since.

As recently as 1991, a German trade magazine ranked New Balance shoes above Asics, Etonic, Karfu, Nike, Reebok, Converse, Lotto and Adidas—all imports. Clearly, New Balance quality is recognized the world over. In fact, in 1991 alone, New Balance exported over 1 million pairs of its athletic shoes to Japan.

New Balance is especially noted for its superior product design. For instance, it was the first company to offer width sizing in athletic shoes and today remains the only major manufacturer to offer it.

New Balance manufactures a complete line of athletic shoes for men and women, including **running, court, cross court, basketball (men only), hiking** and **walking shoes.**

New Balance walking shoes are one of the company's newest product lines and are expected to be the company's second-largest category after running shoes. These walking shoes are made almost exclusively in the U.S. and are a high quality alternative to all-imported Rockports.

Although most New Balance shoes are made in the Boston area or Maine, about 15 percent are imported, so check your labels on these shoes. They sell between $45 and $60 and are available in shoe, sporting and department stores and through the L.L. Bean catalogue.

☎ *(800) 253-SHOE (New Balance)*

*New Balance model 997 men's running shoe*

*New Balance walking shoes*

## Saucony *(Running Shoes Only)*

Almost all Saucony (pronounced "sock-oni") running shoes manufactured by **Hyde Athletic Industries** are made in the U.S. in Bangor, Maine.

Saucony **running shoes** feature a variety of models built on straight, curved or standard lasts (molds) that ensure that Sauconys accommodate a variety of foot shapes and running needs. These shoes cost between $65 and $105 and are available at athletic footwear chains such as *Footlocker* and *Athlete's Foot* and department stores nationwide. Be careful—other types of Saucony athlete's shoes are typically imported.

☎ *(800) 365-7282 (Saucony)*

## Vans *(Fashion Tennis Shoes)*

**Van Doren Rubber** hand makes 100% of its Vans "tennis shoes" in Orange, Calif. The company started out in 1966 manufacturing canvas tennis shoes and selling them directly to the public in its own California stores.

*Women's spring canvas tennis shoes by Vans*

The skateboard craze of the 1970s and an appearance of a pair of black and white checked Vans on movie star Jeff Spicoli in the 1980 hit "Fast Times at Ridgemont High" helped turn Vans into a virtual nationwide craze.

Today, Vans offers a dizzying array of 200 fashionable leisure shoes for women, men, children and infants. From classic deck shoes and slip-ons to trendy high tops and midcut shoes, all Vans combine CVO uppers and thick bottom soles to create the Vans signature look. The shoes come in either canvas or suede and are available in a variety of colors, including brights, earth tones, neutrals, pastels, solids and prints. Or you can custom order a pair of your own design. A basic Vans canvas tennis shoe is a good alternative to all-imported Keds.

Vans are exported to 43 countries. They are available in the U.S. in over 4,600 outlets nationwide and are modestly priced at between $20 and $40.

☎ *(800) VANS-800 (Van Doren)*

## Converse *(Classic Canvas Tennis Shoes Only)*

**Converse** is currently owned by **Interco Inc.** It is no longer much of an American shoe manufacturer. The only models Converse now manufactures in the U.S. are its classic canvas tennis shoes, which are made in Lumberton, N.C.

One of these is the **All Star**, often called the Chuck Taylor, or "chucks." Originally introduced in 1917, this historic piece of American footwear has evolved from a purely functional basketball shoe to a leisure footwear fashion statement available in 56 different colors and styles. By the shoe's 70-year anniversary in 1987, 300 million pairs had been sold around the world.

Converse's more feminine **SkidGrip** basic tie canvas tennis shoes are also made in Lumberton, as are the **Jack Purcell** men's large rubber toe tennis shoes.

## Dexter

The **Dexter Shoe Corp.**, which is the nation's largest privately owned footwear manufacturer, makes **Action Walker** athletic shoes for women.

*Women's Action Walkers by Dexter*

Constructed of soft, lightweight leather with a durable, flexible rubber outsole, these shoes provide superior ventilation and shock absorption to help reduce fatigue when walking.

# Dress Shoes

### Allen Edmonds *(Men's and Women's)*

**Allen-Edmonds Shoe Corp**. of Port Washington, Wis., started making shoes in 1922, when Elbert Allen helped revolutionize the shoe industry by manufacturing shoes without the traditional nails and stiff steel shank. Over the years, the company changed both ownership and focus many times. Today, the company is owned by president John Stollenwerk and 19 employees who saved the company from an out-of-state buyout and possible offshore production in 1989. The company is also the proud manufacturer of some of the finest handcrafted dress shoes in the world.

Allen-Edmonds shoes show up on some of the most famous feet that tread the globe—including President George Bush's. These fine shoes are exported to 33 countries and received the U.S. Commerce Department's "E" award for exporting. Allen-Edmonds even exports to Japan—thanks in part to Stollenwerk's brazen decision to crash a 1987 Tokyo footwear trade show that had denied the company a display booth.

Allen-Edmonds shoes are top quality, classic style dress shoes for both men and women. The men's shoes are handmade from the finest lightweight, supple and breathable leathers and feature the largest array of sizes in the world (size AAAA to EEE and 5 to 18). The shoes also feature the flexibility of a shankless stitched welt design, the comfort and breathability of all leather soles, and a foot-conforming cork insole. The materials and design combine to create an extremely comfortable shoe. Because they are among the best of the best, these shoes carry a fairly hefty price tag. The average cost of a pair of Allen-Edmond's men's shoes is $230 but can go as high as $1,500.

Originally a manufacturer of men's shoes only, Allen-Edmonds began offering women's dress shoes in 1989. The 1992 selection is a wonderful array of classic style, low-heel dress shoes and boots made from the best calfskin, suedes, chamois and exotic leathers available. There are 25 different models, including slip-on, buckle and tie dress shoes as well as more casual yet fashionable boots and demiboots.

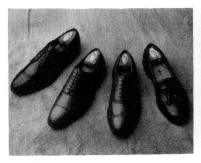 

*Allen-Edmonds men's (l) and women's (r) dress shoes*

Although much of its shoe leather is imported, Allen-Edmonds manufactures every single pair of its shoes with the help of 400 employees in Port Washington and Lake Church, Wis. Allen-Edmonds' shoes can be found at quality department and shoe stores nationwide.

☎ *(414) 284-3461 (Allen-Edmonds)*

## Walk-Over *(Men's and Women's)*

**Walk-Over** is another company that makes all of its high quality men's and women's shoes in the United States (Bridgewater, Mass.). Walk-Over shoes are manufactured by the **Geo. E. Keith Co.**, which has been making shoes in the U.S. since 1758—making it the oldest shoemaker in America.

The company has undergone an incredible turnaround since it was purchased by John S. Thornbeck in 1990. A former Bass and Timberland executive, Thornbeck came to the company with a commitment to continuing Walk-Over's reputation for an extremely high quality shoe. As far as Thornbeck is concerned, the American consumer is ready to replace cheap mass-produced imports with quality shoes, and Walk-Over will answer that need. Says Thornbeck, "I think Walk-Over is a an example of stubborn, crafted quality and of workers skilled enough to rise to the new demand for it."

Walk-Over shoes are made in a unique process called Geo-Welt shoe construction, in which the upper is stitched to the inner sole and base (or welt) of the shoe. It is the highest quality shoe construction possible, and Geo. E. Keith is one of the few remaining U.S. manufacturers to use it. Geo-welt construction provides fit, comfort and durability unequaled by other brands that often simply cement the upper to the sole.

Walk-Over shoes include top quality calfskin dress shoes, Sean and Ryan dress-casual suedes and the basic bucks and saddles that the company is famous for. Prices range from approximately $85 to $180. All Walk-Over shoes offer a great deal of quality and give testament to the company's motto: "Walk-Over shoes are made to a standard, not a price." Although Walk-Over shoes are available at better department and shoe stores nationwide, the company also makes shoes for Cole-Hahn, Banana Republic, L.L. Bean and Lands' End.

☎ *(800) 227-1298 (Walk-Over)*

*Men's and women's dress casual Footwear by Walk Over*

## Dexter *(Men's)*

**Dexter Shoe Co.** manufactures a wide variety of shoes in Maine, including both dress shoes and casual footwear.

Dexter's men's dress **Comfort Classics** combine the comfort and dryness of Dri-Lex® linings with the refined looks of a contemporary dress shoe. Priced under $100, Comfort Classics are also a comfort to the pocketbook.

*Dexter's new Comfort Classics*

## E.T. Wright *(Men's)*

**Executive Shoe Co.** is a family-owned business that celebrated its 100th anniversary in 1991. It is also the producer of "E.T. Wright" American-made men's dress shoes. The only E.T. Wright imports are its high-priced Italian slip-ons which comprise a very small, exclusive portion of its business. The rest of its high quality shoes are manufactured in Bangor, Maine, Carlisle, Pa., and Franklin and Marlington, WV. E.T. Wrights, which retail for $100 to $190, are available in department stores such as Nordstroms and Marshall Fields, or by ordering directly from the company.

☎ *(800) 243-1022. (E.T. Wright)*

## Florsheim *(Men's)*

Although it imports many of its other shoes, **Florsheim Shoe Co.** of Chicago, Ill., makes most of its very fine, classic men's dress shoes in its factories in Michigan, Illinois and Missouri. These shoes are priced at between $80 and $250 and are available at Florsheim and independent shoe stores nationwide.

## Johnston & Murphy *(Men's)*

**Johnston & Murphy** of Nashville, Tenn. was established in 1850, making it one of the oldest shoe manufacturers in the U.S. This company makes the majority (about 85%) of its shoes in

*Johnston & Murphy Georgetown II bal oxfords*

the U.S. in Nashville and Danville, Ky. and Fulton, Miss.

Johnston & Murphy shoes are high-quality, men's dress shoes based on a century and a half of excellence and favored by such discriminating customers as presidents Teddy Roosevelt and Warren Harding. J&M shoes are available at Johnston & Murphy's own shoe stores and better department and specialty stores. Customers may also call and request catalogues and order by mail.

☎ *(800) 424-2854 (J&M)*

## Bostonian *(Men's)*

Bostonian shoes are made by **C&J Clark,** a very large British global footwear manufacturer. However, approximately 80% of Bostonian's men's shoes are made in the U.S. in the company's West Virginia and Pennsylvania factories. Bostonian is best known for its men's dress shoes—the majority of which are made in their U.S. plants. Bostonian men's dress shoes retail for between $100 and $150.

☎ *(800) 999-6780 (Bostonian)*

## Hanover *(Men's)*

Hanover shoes are also manufactured by **C&J Clark**—mostly in the U.S. Although Hanover shoes include **Stetson** and **Sierra** weekend sports shoes and other casual men's footwear, the company is best known for its men's dress shoes and hand-sewn loafers. Hanover shoes are sold only in Hanover shoe stores or by catalogue, a practice that eliminates the middleman and makes these shoes 30%-60% cheaper than most.

☎ *(800) 642-7463 (Hanover)*

## Easy Spirit *(Women's)*

Easy Spirit women's dress shoes are manufactured by **U.S. Shoe Corp**. in Ohio, Indiana and Kentucky. Easy Spirit shoes combine the technology of a walking shoe with the styling of a fashionable pump to create attractive yet extremely comfortable women's heels. These shoes, which "look like a pump yet feel like a sneaker," are available in one to two and a half inch heels in 19 different colors and six different styles. They also come in over 90 widths and sizes to ensure a perfect fit. Sculpted on more footlike, contoured lasts and constructed with a "shock blocker" patented suspension system and the latest in high density, self-renewing foam, these shoes ensure the wearer the ability to walk further and stand longer—in approximately $72 of unrivaled comfort.

☎ *800-EASY-244 (Easy Spirit )*

**Easy Spirt "Daydream" dress pumps**

## Joyce *(Women's)*

Joyce shoes are also manufactured by **U.S. Shoe**. Traditionally known for moderately priced basic pumps, Joyce shoes have recently shifted focus to offer a variety of moderately priced, fashionable dress shoes. Although the traditional pumps are still available and a good buy at around $56 a pair, Joyce shoes now include moderately priced renditions of expensive fashion shoes. These "24-hour shoes" are a bit more versatile than a traditional pump and are priced right at under $50 a pair.

*A sampling of Joyce's new moderately priced fashion shoes*

Some of Joyce's newest shoes are made from a high quality, state-of-the-art synthetic material called chimera, which is virtually indistinguishable from genuine (expensive) kidskin. Joyce's new chimera shoes are targeted at women who avoid leather on principle and those who do not want to pay the high cost of leather.

About 80% of Joyce shoes are made in the U.S.A. in the same Ohio, Indiana and Kentucky factories that make U.S. Shoe's Easy Spirit and Selby brand shoes. All Joyce shoes still come in an extensive variety of widths and sizes and can be found at Joyce-Selby shoe stores and other independent shoe retailers nationwide.

☎ *(800) 284-9928 (Joyce )*

## Lifestride *(Women's)*

**Brown Shoe Co.** of St. Louis, Mo., is the nation's largest domestic manufacturer of footwear. Brown's **Lifestride** dress shoe line, which is 90% made in the U.S., contains contemporary styled dress shoes for the young career woman. U.S.-made Lifestrides are manufactured in Missouri and Tennessee and retail for a moderate $30-$40.

### Naturalizer *(Women's)*

Brown Shoe also makes Naturalizer traditional style dress shoes. Although Naturalizer shoes have been around for 65 years, they remain the best selling women's shoes in the country. Approximately 75% of these $45-$55 shoes are made in the United States in Missouri and Tennessee.

### Selby *(Women's)*

Selby has been making quality women's dress and casual shoes for over 100 years. Once an independent company, Selby is now owned by U.S. Shoe. Selby shoes are fashionable comfort footwear ranging from tailored dress shoes to casual lifestyle shoes. Whatever the model, Selby shoes are renowned for their superior comfort and flexibility—factors that keep Selby customers coming back time and time again. As the company likes to say, "Once you wear a pair of Selbys, you are pretty much a customer for life."

With the exception of its sandals, all Selby shoes are made in the U.S. in Indiana, Ohio and Kentucky. Selby comfort shoes are priced at between $60 and $80 and are available at Joyce-Selby and other shoe stores, department stores and catalogues nationwide.

☎ *(800) 252-SHOE (Selby)*

# Casual shoes

### Dexter *(Men's and Women's)*

One of the best places to look for American-made casual footwear is Dexter Shoe Co. of Dexter, Maine. Dexter has been making every pair of its high quality shoes and boots for men, women and children in Maine since 1957, and has become the largest privately owned shoe manufacturer in the U.S.

Dexter makes an extensive assortment of dress and casual shoes. There are top of the line dress shoes for men including the *Comfort Classic* signature collection discussed earlier. Dexter also makes two top-notch boat shoes—**The Captain**, a high performance boat shoe designed for all types of weather and hardy casual wear, and the ultra-comfortable **Navigator**. Dexter's other offerings include loafers, all weather boots and camp mocs.

*"The Captain" by Dexter*

*Dexter Comfort Collection*

Dexter's shoes for women range from the Venetian style slip-ons found in the **Comfort Collection** to the classic, hand-sewn leather sole **Sporting Life Handsewn Casuals**. Dexter even makes a full range of women's fashion boots. All of Dexter's shoes are priced under $100 and are available at department and shoe stores nationwide.

☎ *(207) 924-5444 (Dexter)*

## Bass *(Men's and Women's)*

**G.H. Bass and Co.** has been making top quality classic style shoes in Wilton, Maine, since 1876.

Although Bass makes a wide variety of footwear today and maintains plants in both Puerto Rico and Brazil, the company still makes most of its well-loved favorites such as its hand-crafted **Weejuns** loafers in Maine.

*Bass women's Weejuns*

These shoes are perhaps the epitome of Bass craftsmanship and durability and "a look that never wears out." Other Bass offering include buc, saddle, outdoor, tailored and sport shoes and **Sunjuns** sandals.

☎ *(800) 950-BASS (Bass)*

## Sebago *(Men's and Women's)*

**Sebago Inc.** makes the vast majority of its quality shoes in Westbrook and Bridgeton, Maine—just as it has been doing for a little under 50 years.

Sebago shoes include its world famous **Docksides** boating moccasins, classic dress loafers and an "Adventure Collection" of sturdy casual outdoor/weekend wear shoes. All Sebago shoes are constructed using a patented welt system in which a flexible leather welt is fastened to the bottom of the shoes for greater support, flexibility and cushioning. Many of them are hand-sewn.

Sebago is a privately owned company that is still run by the founding philosophy, "Every pair crafted with care." Sebagos, especially the 100% American-made **Classic Handsewn Welt Loafers,** are exported to over 50 countries. Sebagos retail for around $100 in the U.S. and can be found at fine shoe, department and outdoor shops.

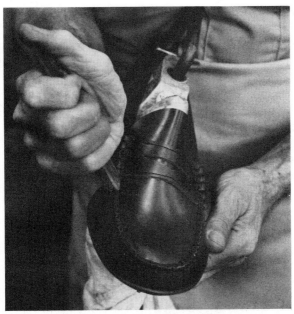

*Careful crafting of a Sebago Classic Handsewn Welt Loafer*

☎ *(207) 854-8474 (Sebago)*

## Timberland

**Timberland** manufactures most of its high quality outdoor style shoes and boots in Mountain City, Tenn., although some items, like its sandals, sneakers and "duck boots," are imported. Timberland shoes and boots are noted for their durability and easy combining of fashion and function. Timberland shoes and boots are typically fairly expensive, but are worth their price in terms of quality and durability.

# Western Boots

The United States is famous for its Western boots, which were created to suit the lifestyle of the American cowboy—thus the name "cowboy boots." Although foreign companies attempt to mimic the Western boot and even import many cheap look-a-likes into the U.S., there is nothing like a U.S. made Western boot.

There are many U.S. companies crafting very fine Western boots in the Southwestern United States. However, there are five manufacturers that seem, by consensus, to be the best of the best. These companies, as well as their parent companies, manufacturing sites and founding dates are listed below.

**Lucchese,** <u>Acme Boot Co.</u>, *El Paso, Tex. (1883)*
**Justin,** <u>Justin Industries</u>, *Fort Worth, Tex. (1879)*
**Nocona,** <u>Justin Industries</u>, *Nocona, Tex. (1925)*
**Tony Lam**a, <u>Justin Industries</u>, *El Paso, Tex. (1911)*
**Dan Post,** <u>The Acme Boot Company</u>, *El Paso, Tex. (1965)*

*Lucchese—*
*The Cadillac of Western Boots*

# Work Shoes and Boots

## Red Wing Shoe Co.

**Red Wing Shoe Co.** of Red Wing, Minn., manufactures a complete line of footwear for the workplace. The company's **Dunoon** shoes are lightweight, ventilated support shoes that make an excellent alternative to all-imported pricey Rockports. All Dunoons feature simple styles and a high level of comfort. They are available in casual, sporty and dress styles and are consequently well-suited to a variety of work (and casual) situations.

Red Wing also makes steel toe and heavy boots and shoes for construction and other dangerous work, shoes designed for service workers and even special electrostatic discharge soled shoes for those working in computer environments. Finally, Red Wing manufactures top quality sport boots under the name "Irish Setter." Where are all these high quality functional shoes made? In Red Wing, Minn., of course. There are over 400 Red Wing Shoe Stores and 4,500 Red Wing retailers across the U.S.

## Weinbrenner

This year, **Weinbrenner Shoe Co.** celebrates 100 years of making top quality work and outdoor footwear in the North Woods of Wisconsin.

Weinbrenner work shoes are made for comfort and job performance. Weinbrenner's **Thorogood** shoes are specially designed for service and uniform personnel, including postal, fire and medical workers. The company also manufactures a complete line of work and safety footwear, including plain and steel toe varieties for construction workers, carpenters and other industrial laborers.

Weinbrenner also makes the **Wood n' Stream** line of boots for outdoor work and leisure, with a new line of hiking boots and shoes.

All Weinbrenner shoes and boots are manufactured in
Merrell and Marshfield Wis. They can be found in uniform
and shoe stores nationwide and through the Penney's, Cabel-
la, Gander Mountain and L.L. Bean catalogues.

# Outdoor Footwear

It is fairly easy to find quality American-made boots for
hunting, fishing and other outdoor activities. However, it can
be nearly impossible to find an American made hiking boot
for walking or hiking. The nation's outdoor stores are
dominated by imported hiking boots by Nike, Asolo, Merrell, Hi-Tec, Vasque, Raichle and others. Consequently, this
section will discuss some of the best U.S.-made outdoor
footwear, with special emphasis on hiking boots.

## Danner

Danner has been making top quality boots in Portland,
Ore., since 1932. Although it originally manufactured work
boots, in the 1960s the company noted the burgeoning national fitness craze and began striving toward the goal of
making the finest outdoor boots possible.

Today, many would say that Danner has reached its goal.
Although the company still offers a line of uniform and work
boots, it also manufactures an extensive assortment of high
quality hunting, fishing and hiking boots—all made in
Portland.

Danner hiking boots include heavy duty leather and
leather/cordura hiking boots for full-pack hiking and the
largest variety of American-made lightweight hiking boots
available.

**Crosshiker** lightweight hiking boots are made of either
leather/cordura nylon or suede/cordura combinations and
are available in a variety of men's and women's styles and a
selection of appealing colors. These boots are perfect for day

hikes or simply kicking around town. Retail prices are $100-$120. Although some of last year's Crosshikers were imported from Taiwan, all 1992 models are American-made.

☎ *(800) 345-0430 (Danner)*

## Rocky Boots

**William Brooks Shoe Co.**, one of the few remaining American family footwear manufacturers, still makes every pair of Rocky boots in Nelsonville, Ohio. It takes over 175 manufacturing steps to hand-craft each pair of Rocky boots, and the folks in Nelsonville take special pride in each and every pair. The result is "the finest boots money can buy."

Rocky **Stalkers** are eight-inch hunting boots that feature leather/cordura uppers, a waterproof Gore-Tex® liner and Thinsulate® thermal insulation. These are lightweight, rugged boots that are extremely comfortable and durable. They are suitable for any outdoor activity and make a great snow boot. Stalkers are available in camouflage or regular uppers and retail for approximately $130.

Rocky also makes **The Scrambler,** a good quality, lightweight hiking boot that features a leather and cordura shell line with a fully waterproof Gore-Tex® bootie. It can be worn for day hiking or backpacking and retails for $110. Steve Newman, the first person to walk around the world solo, wore The Scrambler on his 1982-1986 journey.

## New Balance Hiking Boots

**New Balance Athletic Shoe Co.**, discussed under Athletic shoes, has just introduced a line of American-made hiking boots. New Balance's **MH616** and **WH716** are rugged, durable hiking boots that feature the same lightweight comfort and performance of New Balance's excellent running shoes.

☎ *(800) 253-SHOE (New Balance)*

## L.L. Bean

The L.L. Bean catalogue company offers a variety of American-made outdoor boots and shoes. The company makes many of its own boots in Freeport, Maine, including the legendary **Maine Hunting Shoe**, which gave the company its start. Those shoes that Bean doesn't make are typically obtained from other American manufacturers. For more information on L.L. Bean, please see the Clothing chapter.

☎ *(800) 221-4221 (L.L. Bean)*

*A Danner Crosshiker (l) and "The Scrambler" by Rocky Boots (r)*

*New Balance's new lightweight hiking shoes*

# More Outdoor Footwear Manufacturers

Many of the companies discussed in other sections of this book offer quality boots and shoes designed for outdoor activity. These companies include **Weinbrenner** and **Red Wing** (see Work Shoes and Boots) and **Timberland** (see Casual Shoes).

## Teva Sport Sandals

Although Teva Sport Sandals are hardly an outdoor boot, they are a widespread favorite of those active in the out-of-doors. There is hardly a boatsman or serious camper in the U.S. who would dream of spending a summer without a pair of Tevas.

*Teva Sport Sandals*

Tevas are manufactured by **Deckers Corp.** in Carpinteria, Calif. The company was founded in 1982 by Grand Canyon raft guide Mark Thatcher, who personally designed the sandals.

Although initially popular only among so-called "river rats" (canoeists, kayakers and rafters), Tevas have become a must-have among outdoor enthusiasts and street-walking cityfolk alike.

These unique sandals feature adjustable Velcro straps, an open or closed toe design, terrific traction (wet or dry) and unusual stability. In fact, some people actually jog in their Tevas. Not only are Tevas perfect for all types of boating, but they can be used for any number of outdoor activities. Tevas retail for about $45 a pair and are so durable that they are well worth the investment. Teva Sport Sandals for adults and children can be found at outdoor and wilderness stores nationwide or can be ordered through the L.L. Bean catalogue.

# Children's Shoes

American-made children's shoes are difficult to find. Children tend to favor athletic type shoes such as Nikes, Reebok and L.A. Gear. Unfortunately, this type of shoe is almost always an import. However, American manufacturers still make a number of high quality children's shoes—particularly in the dress and dress casual categories.

## Dexter

**Dexter** makes American-made children's boat shoes and ankle boots.

☎ *(207) 924-5444 (Dexter)*

## Kepner-Scott

Kepner-Scott makes all of its boys' and girls' leather shoes in Orwigsburg, Pa. Kepner-Scott leather shoes come in dress styles such as patent leather, schoolshoes such as oxfords and dress-casual "Sunday-Monday" shoes, which are appropriate for a variety of settings. Kepner-Scott also offers a full line of toddlers' "first steppers," boots and dress shoes.

☎ *(717) 366-0229 (Kepner-Scott)*

## Minnetonka

The **Minnetonka** company produces moccasins for children and infants (adults, too) in the U.S. Commonwealth of Puerto Rico.

☎ *(612) 331-8493 (Minnetonka)*

## Sebago

Sebago makes a complete line of American-made boys' and girls' penny loafers and boat shoes.

☎ *(207) 854-8474 (Sebago)*

## Stride Rite

**Stride Rite** makes some of its shoes for boys and girls in the U.S.

## Vans

**Vans** manufactures fashionable tie and velcro tennis shoes in a variety of colors and patterns for children and infants.

These all-American-made shoes are not only fashionable and fun, but a wonderful replacement for the large number of imported children's athletic shoes on the market. Please see the Vans section under Athletic Shoes for more information.

☎ *(800) VANS-800 (Van Doren)*

*Vans' boys' "Cavewriting" and "Confusion" tennis-shoes*

## Willits

Willits makes leather children's shoes for boys and girls in Halifax, Pa.

☎ *(800) 544-3633 (Willits)*

# 3

# Bicycles

## The Industry

Bicycling is one of the most popular activities in the United States. According to the latest industry figures, there are approximately 90 million cyclists in the U.S.—with more added every day. Americans cycle for exercise and leisure. Some are casual riders, others race or use their bicycles to tour or vacation. Many commute to work. The newest and most rapidly growing type of cycling is off-road, or "mountain biking."

Whatever their cycling habits, U.S. consumers purchased $3.3 billion of bicycles and related parts and accessories in 1990. About half of these sales were for imported bicycles and related goods. Taiwan is the major source of imported bicycles, with seven out of 10 imported bikes coming from that nation. China recently replaced Korea as the second-biggest importer. Together, China, Korea and Taiwan account for 92% of all bicycles imported to the U.S.

Following a period in the 1980s in which imports dominated the market, U.S. bicycle manufacturers are now holding their ground. Although competition remains fierce, by 1990 U.S. manufacturers had regained a 55% share of the U.S. bicycle market. In 1990, domestic bicycle manufacturing increased by 12.4% over 1989 and 6.5% over the average of the previous 10 years. In contrast, imports fell 10% in 1990 but were still greater than the average of the past 10 years.

# Understanding the U.S. Market

The bicycle market is complex. It includes bikes for both children and adults and everything from inexpensive mass-produced steel bicycles to custom designed, hand-built machines crafted from high tech materials and costing thousands of dollars. Many historically American companies now produce the bulk of their bicycles abroad. Other manufacturers produce some bikes (usually upper-end) in the U.S. and import the rest. Many companies design bicycles here but manufacture them abroad. This is especially true in the field of mountain, or all-terrain bicycles (ATBs).

The mountain bike, designed for "off-road" riding with its wide, knobby tires, a smaller frame, extensive gearing systems and straight handlebars, was an American innovation that has taken the world by storm. Today, mountain bikes are purchased for not only trail riding but city and even touring uses as well. Hybrid bicycles, which combine the features of mountain bikes and bicycles designed for pavement (road bikes), are another American-led innovation that is extremely popular.

As with many industries, American design and pioneering does not always result in American manufacturing—the majority of U.S.-designed mountain bikes and hybrids, not to mention road bikes, are manufactured abroad. Don't be fooled by a bicycle marked "designed in the U.S.A."—this is a sure sign that bicycle is manufactured out of the country. Otherwise, it would say "made" or "manufactured" in the U.S.

# American-Made Bicycles

Despite these complexities, there is an American-made bicycle for every taste, riding level and budget. It should be noted that every American-built bicycle includes a large number of imported components such as rims, tires, brakes, cranksets and derailleurs. Unfortunately, domestic component manufacturers simply do no exist in the scope and price range required for mass production. In fact, two companies, Shimano and Suntour of Japan, currently supply the majority of the world's quality bicycle components.

All of the bicycles we have chosen consist of American-manufactured frames (the most important part of any bicycle) equipped with largely imported components. These bicycles represent not only the best in American-made quality, but the most "American" bicycles you can purchase.

# Moderately Priced Bicycles

Moderately priced bicycles tend to contain more American-made components than their higher priced counterparts. This is because these companies make some of their own components, such as rims.

## Huffy

**Huffy Corp.** is the nation's largest bicycle manufacturer. It is also the most efficient manufacturer of bicycles in the entire world. Huffy's factory is in Celinas, Ohio (just outside Dayton), can produce a bike with only 45 minutes of direct labor. This is one-third to one-quarter the time needed by the Taiwanese.

Huffy produces bicycles in nearly every category. Huffy has a full line of children's bicycles, including the radio equipped "Street Rockers" pictured below. For older children and teenagers, Huffy makes a variety of slightly more expensive BMX (motocross) and ATB models. For adults, Huffy offers hybrid street bicycles, road and mountain bikes and popular replicas of "old-fashioned" one speed "cruisers." All Huffy bicycles are moderately priced. Children's bicycles sell for under $100, while adult bicycles are typically under $150.

Although Huffy's position as a mass market retailer has caused many to belittle the quality of its products, this reputation is not accurate. Huffy also makes a small line of world class racing bikes called "Tritons" at its Dayton Technical Development Center. The American bicycles for the 1984 and 1988 Olympics were designed and built at this same center. According to Huffy, much of the technological innovation needed to produce Huffy's world class racing bicycles has filtered down to Huffy's mass production models.

Huffy bicycles are available through Kmart, Toys-R-Us, Childworld, Children's Palace, Lionel Kiddie City and the Sears catalogue.

☎ *(800) USA-BIKE (Huffy)*

**The 26262 Crosswind by Huffy**

*Boys' radio-equipped "Street Rocker" by Huffy*

## Murray

**Murray Ohio Manufacturing Co.** is another large manufacturer of moderately priced bicycles for children and adults. At one time, the company tried moving its manufacturing operations abroad, but it found it could produce a better bike in the United States. Although Murray bicycles contain a relatively high percentage of American parts and are assembled in Lawrenceburg, Tenn., Murray has been owned by the British concern **Tomkins P.L.C.** since 1988.

Murray bicycles include mountain (or ATB) bicycles, road bikes and a new line of hybrids, which combine the best features of both mountain and road bikes. Murray also offers a wide selection of "cruiser" bicycles like the one pictured below.

All Murray bicycles are made of steel alloy and are under $250. The average price of an adult bike is $140; a child's bike $80. Murray bicycles can be found at J.C. Penney, Kmart, Toys-R-Us, Wal-Mart and other national retailers.

☎ *(800) 251-8007 (Murray)*

*A Murray "Monterey" cruiser*

## Roadmaster

**Roadmaster Corp.** has been manufacturing Roadmaster bicycles in the U.S. since 1951. Roadmaster makes ATBs and hybrid bicycles for adults along with a large selection of children's bicycles. Road-master offers something for every age child, including tricycles, bicycles with train-ing wheels and sidewalk and BMX bicycles for older boys and girls.

*A Roadmaster Deluxe Duo-Deck tricycle*

Although Roadmaster imports a few of its all-terrain bikes, about 90% of Roadmaster's bikes are made here in the

U.S. in Olney, Ill., and Delavan, Wis. These bicycles are easy to pick out because they display a "made in the U.S." decal.

Roadmaster bicycles are very reasonably priced and are available at Wal-Mart, Best Products, Montgomery Ward, AAFES and Bradlees.

☎ *(800) 626-2811 (Roadmaster)*

*A pair of Roadmaster sidewalk bikes*

# More Expensive Bicycles

## Cannondale

If you are interested in purchasing an American-made, finely crafted bicycle, **Cannondale Corp.** of Georgetown, Conn., is your best source. Unlike many of its competitors, Cannondale makes every single one of its bicycles distributed in the U.S. in its plants in Bedford and Phillipsburg, Pa. (Cannondale recently opened a Holland assembly plant that uses frames exported from the U.S.)

Cannondale began just 20 years ago with president and founder Joe Montgomery and four staffers hand-building bicycle trailers in a crowded loft above a pickle factory. A year later, this small group began to hand-build bicycles. Although Cannondale has grown significantly since its humble beginnings, Joe Montgomery's commitment to quality, innovation and a hand-built bicycle remains to this day.

The quality of Cannondales has brought the company wild success. Besides being chosen as one of *Bicycle Magazine's* hottest bicycles in '91 and '92, Cannondales are ridden by the likes of Madonna, Speaker of the House Tom Foley and members of the New York Giants. Cannondales are also exported all over the world, including Japan.

Cannondale can hardly keep up with the demand for its bikes. In fact, Cannondale had already sold out of much of its 1992 production by January. Although such high demand sometimes leave customers waiting, these bikes are worth it.

Cannondale bicycles feature patented, wide-girth, all-aluminum frames that make these bikes lighter, more efficient and more shock absorbing than a traditional steel frame bicycle. Cannondale was the first company to mass produce such a frame. Each Cannondale frame is computer designed and hand-built. It takes four hours and 40 pairs of human hands to manufacture a single Cannondale frame. Furthermore, every Cannondale frame carries a lifetime guarantee.

Cannondale bicycles include a range of selections in all terrain bicycles, including award-winning suspension mountain bikes, racing bikes, touring bikes and cross-training bicycles. Cannondale also makes an excellent tandem. These bikes are priced from $600 to $2,750 and are available in bicycle shops nationwide.

The Pennsylvania plants also churn out a variety of high-quality bicycling accessories, including men's and women's cycling clothing, racks, packs, child-toting trailers, water bottles and water bottle holders. This year, Cannondale is selling a special "Rails to Trails" water bottle. For every one of these sold, Cannondale will donate 50 cents to the national

Rails to Trails Conservancy, a non-profit organization that converts abandoned railways into trails for cycling, hiking and other activities.

☎ *(800) BIKE-USA (Cannondale)*

*A Cannondale H-800 cross-training bicycle*

*Cannondale's 2.8 Series racing bicycle*

*Cannondale's Delta V suspension mountain bike*

## Trek U.S.A.

**Trek U.S.A.** is another U.S. company committed to manufacturing bicycles in the U.S. Although Trek imports its low-end mountain and hybrid bikes, the company espouses a commitment to U.S. labor and U.S. products. As a Trek spokesperson explained, "We are very committed both to the labor market here in the U.S. and offering consumers in the U.S. and worldwide a quality made-in-the-U.S.A. product... We are aware of the implications of creating jobs and fueling the economy."

In fact, Trek used to make some of its road bikes overseas but has shifted production of these bikes back to the U.S. As of 1992, all Trek **road bikes** will be made in Waterloo, Wis. Trek also makes its upper-end mountain bikes with series numbers above 850, and upper-end cross hybrids with series numbers higher than 730 in the U.S. However, Trek's new line of family-targeted bicycles, marketed under the "Jazz" label, are produced overseas.

Trek bicycles include frames made from a variety of materials such as steel and aluminum alloys and the cutting edge technology of carbon fiber. Trek road bikes are priced from $425 and include both racing and touring style bicycles from 12 to 21 speeds. Trek bicycles are available at bicycle shops nationwide.

☎ *(800) 522-8739 (Trek)*

*A Trek road sport/touring bicycle*

## Haro

Haro Bicycles, a division of the British **Derby Cycle Corp.** makes five out of eight of its custom quality bike models in its plant in Seattle, Calif. All of its children's bicycles are imported. U.S.-made Haro bicycles are constructed of steel and aluminum alloys, are all-terrain style and retail for $350 to $2,600.

## Raleigh

**Raleigh** started out as a small British company on Raleigh Street in Nottingham, England, in 1887. Raleigh only began producing bicycles in the U.S. in 1982, when it sold Huffy Corp. the rights to manufacture and distribute Raleigh bicycles in the U.S. These rights are currently held by **Derby Cycle Corp.** of Britain.

For the most part, U.S.-made Raleigh bicycles are upper-end, more expensive ones that feature a state-of-the-art aluminum composite frame, what Raleigh calls its **Technium® bicycles.** These bicycles are made in Kent, Wash., outside Seattle. The Kent plant also manufactures a fair amount of more moderate chrome-moly frame bicycles. Again, most low-end models, including all Raleigh's children's bicycles are imported. U.S.-made Raleigh's start at around $300 and include road, mountain and hybrid bicycles. Technium bicycles start at around $600.

☎ *(800) 222-5527 (Raleigh)*

## Schwinn

**Schwinn Cycling and Fitness** currently limits its U.S. production to custom-built all-terrain and road racing bicycles that are priced from $750. These bikes are made in Waterford, Wis., and must be special ordered through your nearest Schwinn dealer.

## Specialized

Although **Specialized Bicycle Component** put out the first production (or assembly line) all-terrain bicycle in the world and designs its ATBs here in the U.S., the vast majority of Specialized bicycles are made in Taiwan and Japan. In 1992, the only Specialized models made in the U.S., in Morgan Hill, Calif., are the top of the line "M2" bicycle and frame set (from $1,200) and the "Specialized Carbon Bike" model, formerly called the Stumpjumper Epic (from $3,200).

# The Cream of the Crop

There are a multitude of small bicycle companies producing custom-built or custom quality bicycles for serious enthusiasts and racers all over the world. These operations range from a single innovator building a few bikes a year in a garage to small production companies. In any case, these state-of-the-art bicycle producers are absolutely some of the best in the entire world. They also carry pretty hefty price tags. What follows is a list of the best and most well known of these premier U.S. bicycle manufactures.

## Fat City

**Fat City Bicycle Co.** makes all of its bicycles in Somerville, Mass. Fat City makes steel mountain and road bikes of custom-built quality that sell for $1400 and up and that are exported all over the world, including Germany, Japan and Italy.

# Klein

**Klein Bicycle Co.** of Chehalis, Wash. is one of the largest producers of custom quality bicycles in the U.S. Klein specializes in hand-built aluminum frame bicycles. In fact, when Gary Klein built an aluminum frame bicycle as part of an entrepreneurial project at MIT, he was the first person in the world to do so and spearheaded a virtual revolution in the bicycling industry. Thanks to Klein, bicycle manufacturers around the globe now use aluminum and aluminum composites to manufacture bicycle frames.

Despite the spread of this technology, Klein remains widely regarded as the world's best manufacturer of all-aluminum frame bicycles.

*The Klein Pinnacle*

One testament to Klein quality is the fact that its bicycles are exported to 33 foreign countries including Japan. Klein bicycles have also been ridden by both the 1991 and 1992 world champions in women's downhill mountain biking.

Klein frames are hand-built in Chehalis, Wash. and are available in road, mountain and cross-bike models. One of Klein's most popular models is **The Pinnacle** mountain bike pictured above. This bicycle retails for $1,200.

To purchase a Klein bicycle or simply order a Klein frame and build it with your own choice of components, visit one of 700 Klein dealers nationwide.

## Manitou

**Manitou** is a very small producer of hand-built mountain bikes. Company founder Douglas Bradbury builds every Manitou bicycle himself in Colorado Springs, Colo.

Manitou mountain bikes feature lightweight frames made from Easton VARI-LITE 7000 aluminum tubing. Although Bradbury puts out only about 100 $5,000 bicycles a year, his bicycles are demanded by serious enthusiasts and racers all over the world. Of last year's allotment of Manitous, one-third were exported to Europe and another third to Japan.

## Ritchey

**Ritchey** produces custom quality ATB and road bikes in Redwood City, Calif. Top of the line Ritcheys are built from start to finish in Redwood and start at $2,400. All other Ritchey bicycles include approximately 40%-50% U.S. production, including assembly and welding of imported frame pieces. Ritchey, which was one of the forerunners in the ATB revolution, also manufactures components such as rims and handlebars, as well as clothing, in the U.S.

## Serotta

**Serotta Sports** made its reputation as a producer of fine road bikes. Serious bicycle enthusiasts all over the world are addicted to these bicycles. Serotta bicycles are manufactured in Middle Grove, N.Y., and cost between $1,700 and $4,000.

## Titan

**Titan** is one of the smaller custom quality bicycle producers. Begun in 1981, Titan currently turns out only 300-400 bicycles a year. Titan bicycles are of the ATB and

BMX (motocross) variety and feature titanium frame construction. They retail for $575 to $2,600.

# Components

Although the vast majority of bicycle components are imported, there are U.S. component manufacturers. Most of them are small custom producers. These companies manufacture specialized state-of-the-art components that are usually quite expensive and are targeted at racers looking for top quality components.

## Sun

**Sun Metal Products Inc.** manufactures a full range of alloy and steel rims in Warsaw, Ind. Sun Metal's rims are sold under four different brand names. **Sun** rims and steel spoke wheels are designed for moderately priced bicycles and often appear as original equipment on Huffy and Murray bicycles. Sun **Chinook** aluminum rims are designed for off-road bicycles and are original equipment on many top-of-the-line ATBs including Cannondale's "V-2" and Raleigh's Technium "Peak." **Mistral** is Sun's racing and performance line of aluminum rims. **Levanter** brand aluminum rims are Sun's newest line. These rims are designed for manufacturers of more expensive and custom quality bicycles.

Sun Metal Products is one of the few surviving companies in the U.S. metal fabrication industry and one of a handful of U.S. bicycle rim manufacturers. Interestingly enough, a few years back Sun arranged to have some of its alloy rims made in Taiwan. However, the Taiwanese plant was unable to produce the volume or quality that Sun required, and Sun quickly moved those operations back to the states. Sun rims and wheels can be purchased through bicycle shops nationwide.

## Bullseye

**Bullseye** makes state of the art cranks and other components in Burbank, Calif.

## Cook Brothers

**Cook Brothers** makes aluminum cranks, stems, hubs and bottom brackets in Santa Ana, Calif.

## Ringle

**Ringle Components** of Trenton, N.J. makes lightweight titanium quick release skewers and seat posts from both aluminum and titanium. They also make lightweight hubs and an anti-chain suck device.

# ★☆ 4 ☆★
# Motorcycles

## The Industry

At one time, there were more than 300 U.S. companies producing motorcycles in the U.S. In 1992, there are two: Harley-Davidson—legendary producer of some of the world's best motorcycles—and Buell Motor Co.—a new company that has set out to manufacture an all-American sport bike.

## Harley-Davidson

Harley-Davidson motorcycles are renowned not only for their performance and quality but for the unique feeling that comes with owning a "Harley." Remember the film *Easy Rider*, "Get your motor runnin'/ Headin' out on the highway/ Looking for adventure"? Peter Fonda's motorcycle of choice in that classic film was Harley-Davidson, of course.

The biggest testament to the quality of Harleys is the loyalty of those who ride them. Harley customers are some of the most devoted in the business. Then there are the exports. Harley-Davidson motorcycles are exported to 35 different countries, including Japan, Australia and Europe. Another tribute to Harley-Davidson quality is the fact that their motorcycle designs are copied the world over.

## Modern Harleys

Following a troubling period in the 1970s when Harley-Davidson was bought by American Machine and Foundry and quality was sacrificed for quantity, 13 Harley-Davidson executives bought the company in 1981 and returned it to its historic commitment to quality and customer satisfaction.

Consequently, modern Harleys are some of the best ever. One of the first changes of the new owners was the development of a new "V2 Evolution" engine, which quickly became the mainstay of the Harley line. The company also improved the gearbox and engine mounting to reduce vibration and produce a smoother ride. These technical improvements, combined with other design and production organization changes, allowed Harley to significantly decrease manufacturing costs and production time, while dramatically increasing quality and reliability.

Harley-Davidson's commitment to better quality did not stop with these initial efforts. Since 1989, the company has spent approximately $80 million on new, product-enhancing equipment—just about the same amount the executives paid for the company in 1981. One of these sweeping capital improvements is Harley-Davidson's all-new $23 million paint center.

The best part of Harley-Davidson improvements is that they are consumer-driven. Harley-Davidson executives attend motorcycle rallies and other Harley gatherings across the country to listen to Harley owners' needs and suggestions.

## Harley-Davidson 1992

In 1992, Harley-Davidson is offering 20 different models. All are the combination of classic styling and modern computer-aided design, or CAD, which modern Harley owners have come to expect.

In addition, the entire 1992 line has undergone significant improvements, including new brake and disc material for improved brake lever effort, continuously vented fuel tanks for smooth fuel delivery to the carburetor and a new powder coat clear paint for a strong, baked-on clear finish.

## Sportster®

Sporster models are the smallest that Harley makes. Introduced in 1957, the legendary Sportster models feature 883cc or 1200cc (one model) engines and a five-speed transmission. The XHL Sportster 883 makes a great, modestly priced "no frills, all thrills" bike for first-time riders.

*The Harley-Davidson XLH Sportster 883*

## Dyna Glide™

Introduced in 1991, the **Dyna Glide (FXD)** series is Harley's newest product line. These finely crafted motorcyles combine the original, rigid-mounted H-D Low Rider motorcycles of the late 1970s with the handling and rubber-isolated ride of today's Low Riders. This unique combination is created by an internal steel frame chassis with a single backbone that uses a two-point, rubber engine isolation mounting system. The Dyna Glide series was also H-D's first series to be designed from the ground up using CAD.

*The Harley-Davidson FXDC Dyna Glide Custom*

## Softail®

The Softail (FX/FL) series reproduces the nostalgic look of a "hardtail" (a motorcycle that has no rear suspension), but not the "hard" ride. This is achieved by two horizontally mounted, adjustable gas-charged shocks hidden beneath the frame. All Softail models have 1340cc engines, five-speed transmissions and belt final drives, and are available with either 16-or 21-inch front wheels.

## Touring

Harley-Davidson's **Touring (FL)** series offers some of the best touring motorcycles on the planet. From the no-frills FLHS Electra Glide Sport to the incredible FLTC Tour Glide Ultra Classic, Harley's touring models' original equipment includes air-adjustable, anti-dive front suspensions, air-adjustable rear suspensions, rider and passenger floorboards and saddlebags. Although the number of amenities varies from model to model, these motorcycles are all designed with the long haul in mind.

*The Harley-Davidson FLTC-Tour Glide Ultra Classic*

## Sidecars

Harley is the only major motorcycle manufacturer to make its own sidecars. Harley make three different models—one for Low Rider (FXR) motorcycles with tall suspensions and two for the Touring series.

## The Harley Owner's Group

One final Harley benefit to keep in mind is that every new Harley-Davidson motorcycle comes with a free one-year membership in its national club—the *Harley Owner's Group,* or *HOG.*

Harley-Davidson is headquartered in Milwaukee, Wis. Although it manufactures its engines and other components in Milwaukee and Tomohawk, Wis., its motorcycles are assembled in York, Pa., and prototype-tested in Talledega, Ala. Harley estimates the American component content of its bikes to be approximately 90%.

# Buell Motor Co.

So you thought Harley-Davidson motorcycles were the only all-American motorcycles? Think again. A small company in Mukwonago, Wis., has quietly been producing top-of-the-line sport motorcycles for five years. Buell Motor Co. was founded in 1987 by former Harley-Davidson engineer and professional road racer Erik Buell.

From the beginning, Buell's mission was to offer an American sport bike that would put a dent in the Japanese and European dominated sport bike market. Progressing from a "backyard shop" and a staff of five to the current 19 employees and an output that has multiplied eight times, Buell is well on his way.

Although the current output of 200 motorcycles a year and a $16,000-a-bike price tag makes Buell a small, custom producer, Buell has larger aspirations. Eventually, Buell would like to produce sport bikes for the mass market. Erik Buell sees the continued expansion of Buell Motors as fulfilling a twofold dream—to build a top quality American sport bike and to employ Americans. As he admits, "I am obsessed with the whole idea of putting Americans to work."

Buell motorcycles are unique. They are a heady combination of sleek, aerodynamic design and rider-friendly comfort.

## RS1200 WestWind

The latest Buell design is the RS1200 WestWind. The WestWind is powered by a 1200cc Harley-Davidson Evolution® engine with a five-speed transmission. Other features include a patented Uniplanar® rubber-mounted isolation engine system, a Chrome-Moly triangulated space frame and Kevlar reinforced fiberglass body panels. The WestWind's front suspension system uses an inverted-fork design—something that has never been used on a street bike before.

*A Buell RSS 1200*

As the RSS 1200 amply illustrates, Buells are designed to be beautiful—even artistic—bikes that are guaranteed to turn heads and invoke envy from BMW and Italian sport bike owners alike.

Buell motorcycles are built from American components in Mukwonago, Wis., just outside Milwaukee. In fact, Buell claims the highest U.S. content in the industry with approximately 95% U.S.-made components. Buells are available at over 100 Buell dealers nationwide.

# Foreign Motorcycles Made in the USA

The biggest sellers in the American market are all foreign: Honda, Yamaha, Suzuki and Kawasaki. Both Honda and Kawasaki manufacture motorcycles in the United States.

## American-Made Hondas

**Honda** manufactures some of its motorcyles in Marysville, Ohio. (This is the same site where Honda manufactures some of its car models.) All Honda **Gold Wings** are made in Marysville. These motorcycles are large, six-cyclinder touring motorcycles, which are quite popular in the U.S. Interestingly enough, Gold Wings are exported from Marysville to 30 different countries—including Japan. Honda also makes its V-twin cruiser, the **Shadow 1100**, in the U.S. Finally, Honda makes most of its **ATV** models in Marysville, including the Four Tracks 300 4x4 and the Four Tracks 300, 200 and 90.

## American-Made Kawasakis

Kawasaki claims to be the first foreign vehicle manufacturer to set up shop in the United States back in 1974. Kawasaki maintains a factory in Lincoln, Neb. This plant produces Kawasaki's Police Special motorcycles and all of its ATVs. It also produces the ZX600c, ZX600D, VN750A, ZX1100C, ZG1000A and ZG1200B motorcycles.

Although Kawasaki manufactures engines for some of its vehicles in a separate plant in Maryville, Mo., some of these bikes contain imported engines. So if you are set on buying an American-made Kawasaki, be prepared to ask a lot of questions regarding the production of the motorcycle you are interested in.

# ★☆ 5 ☆★
# Tires

## The Industry

In the past few years, the U.S. tire industry has undergone some tough times. Many U.S. firms were taken over by foreign interests. Although Goodrich and Uniroyal attempted to stave off foreign takeover by merging, the French tire maker Michelin bought out Uniroyal-Goodrich in 1989. That same year, Firestone was acquired by the Japanese tire company Bridgestone. Of the four previously "great" American manufacturers—Firestone, Uniroyal, Goodyear and Goodrich—only Goodyear remains American-owned. To make matters worse, the tire industry has been in a significant slump as a result of both the ailing U.S. car industry and the struggling U.S. economy.

## Shopping for American-Made Tires

When the tread on your tires is down to a quarter of an inch or less, it is time to replace them. But it can be difficult to determine which replacement tires are American-made. Foreign companies such as Dunlop, Bridgestone, Michelin and Perelli make tires in the U.S., while U.S.-Goodyear makes some tires in France or Germany. Tires on the U.S. market originate from all over the world.

To be sure a tire is made in the U.S., check the country of origin often marked on the side of the tire. To cut your shopping time in half, look for **Goodyear** and **Cooper** tires.

These two companies make the best American-made tires manufactured by American-owned companies.

# Goodyear

**Goodyear Tire & Rubber Co.** is the indisputable quality leader in the world tire industry. The Akron, Ohio based company is also the last major American-owned tire company and one of only two remaining U.S. tire manufacturers still publicly traded and American owned. Although Goodyear does produce tires abroad, almost every Goodyear tire sold in the United States is manufactured in one of its Tennessee, Oklahoma, North Carolina, Illinois, Texas, Virginia, Kentucky, Kansas or Alabama plants.

The fact that Goodyear tires are chosen as the original equipment on many new cars is a testament to Goodyear quality. Many car companies wouldn't dream of putting out a new model without a set of Goodyear tires on it. Goodyear tires are original equipment on many prestigious American sports cars including the Corvette ZR-1. Even Japanese automakers in the U.S. have selected Goodyear tires for their performance cars, including the Lexis SC 400.

Goodyear also makes excellent replacement tires. Although tires can be difficult to shop for because not every tire comes in a size that will fit your car or truck, there is generally a Goodyear replacement tire for every vehicle.

## Goodyear High- Performance Auto Tires

Without a doubt, Goodyear's **Eagle** line is the world's best-selling high-performance brand. Because of its involvement in nearly every racing venue, the company has transferred technological know-how from the racetrack to the tires consumers use for their own vehicles. The Goodyear **Eagle GS** family of tires is Goodyear's newest contribution to performance tire technology.

The Eagle GS-C offers the ultimate combination of wet and dry road performance with a directional, asymmetric tread design, which has more tread on the tire's outside shoulder for improved cornering power. Eagle GS-C tires are original equipment on the 1992 Corvette LT-1 and ZR-1 models. The Eagle GS-D, which also has a directional tread design, is the aggressive heir to Goodyear's famous "Gator-back" tire. The Eagle GS-A asymmetric tire is specifically tuned to complement the ultra-high-performance Ferrari F40.

Goodyear's other high-performance radials include the sporty, speed-rated **Eagle VR**, the high-performance all-weather **Eagle GT+4**, the luxurious **Eagle GA** touring radial, the dependable, durable **Eagle GT**, the price conscious **Eagle ST** and the high-performance mud and snow **Eagle M+S**.

## Goodyear All-Season Auto Tires

Goodyear introduced an exciting all-season radial in 1991—the **Aquatred**. This new tire features a deep ridge, or Aquachannel, that runs around the center of the tire. Side tread channels work with the Aquachannel to spew water out the sides and rear of the tire—making this tire resistant to hydroplaning and other wet driving dangers. The Aquatred has been called revolutionary by the media and has received engineering and design awards.

Another Goodyear radial that was introduced in 1991 is the **Invicta GFE**. This "green" tire is engineered to cut tire/road friction (rolling resistance) and consequently reduce fuel consumption and related exhaust emissions by about 4%. The Invicta GTE combines fuel efficiency and environmental consciousness with excellent wear, grip and performance and may save the consumer up to half its initial cost.

Goodyear's other radial tires include the quiet-riding, long-wearing **Invicta GS**, the advanced tread rib **Invicta GL**, the reliable traction **S4S**, the steel-belted **Tiempo**, the metric-sized **T-Metric** and the price conscious **Decathlon**.

*Goodyear's new deep channel Aquatred tire*

## Goodyear Truck and RV Tires

Goodyear's tire expertise does not stop at the family sedan. Goodyear makes the **Wrangler** line of tires for pickup trucks, four-wheelers, sport utility vehicles, vans, RVs and tractor trailors.

Wrangler tires are available in seven different models— each designed for a specific highway or off-road application. All Wrangler tires feature extra deep tread for superior traction in all sorts of demanding situations. In fact, the presidential Lincoln limousine is outfitted with a custom set of Wrangler tires, just in case there is an emergency need to drive in snow or mud.

For the multipurpose vehicle owner, Goodyear recently introduced the **Wrangler GS-A**. The GS-A is the first Wrangler tire to feature an asymmetric tread design. The GS-A also has the deepest grooves of any Wrangler tire for excellent wet road handling and a rugged tread compound for longer tire life.

Goodyear's **Unisteel** tractor trailer tires are unmatched for durability and ride. Since Goodyear is North America's largest retreader and its casings set the industry standard, Goodyear is also the best place to go when your Unisteels wear out.

## Other Goodyear Brand Names

In 1992, Goodyear exited the private brand tire business to focus attention on the Goodyear brand name. However, **Kelly-Springfield Tire Co.**, a subsidiary of Goodyear since 1935, makes **Kelly** and many private label replacement tires in Cumberland, Md.

Private label Kelly-Springfield tires include **Douglas, Hallmark, Lee, Monarch, Montgomery-Ward, Sears, Shell** and **Star**. Most of these labels also have other companies manufacturing tires for them—including those that manufacture offshore.

To find out if a tire sold under one of the above labels is a U.S.-made Kelly tire, look at the DOT code on the sidewall of the tire. If the code begins with a PJ, MM, PK, MN, PL, MP, PT, PU, PY or TA the tire is an American-made Kelly-Springfield.

# Cooper

**Cooper Tire & Rubber Co.** of Findlay, Ohio, is the only U.S. tire manufacturer besides Goodyear to remain a publicly traded American-owned tire company. Cooper makes tires exclusively for the replacement market. In the past few years, Cooper has been quite an American manufacturing success story. Despite an industry slump, Cooper's emphasis on the replacement market has resulted in soaring profits and market share—and a position as the ninth largest and one of the most profitable tire makers in the world. Founded in Akron, Ohio, in 1914, Cooper relocated to a vacant factory in Findlay in 1917. Cooper makes all of its tires in manufacturing facilities in Ohio, Mississippi, Arkansas and Georgia. The Cooper business philosophy is to offer a fairly priced quality tire and superior customer service. The company does a fine job of both.

Cooper tires are a great deal—they are well-made, moderately priced, dependable and 100% made in the U.S.A. Cooper offers a full tire line, including passenger, light truck and medium truck tires, in a variety of styles and sizes. Cooper tires can be found through independent tire dealers under the Cooper brand or under private labels such as **Falls Mastercraft, Dean, Eldorado** and **Atlas**.

☎ *(800) 854-6288 (Cooper)*

# Coker Antique Tires

Joseph "Corky" Coker took over the vintage tire division of his father's Coker Tire in 1974. Since then, **Coker Tire** has become synonymous with the world's best and most authentic vintage tires for cars, trucks, motorcycles, bicycles and even airplanes. It is not surprising then, that Coker vintage tires are shipped to every state in the U.S. and are exported to 27 foreign countries as diverse and far-flung as Britain, South Africa and Japan.

Coker Tire is headquartered in Chattanooga, Tenn. The company has spent a great deal of effort either tracking down and buying or recreating the molds used to make its antique tires. Although Coker owns the molds for its tire lines, the company basically acts as a distributor and licenses a range of companies to manufacture its tires.

Although some of its molds are positioned in foreign countries, 90% of Coker's vintage tires are manufactured in small U.S. tire factories like *McReary Tire and Rubber* of Indiana, Pa., or *Denman Tire and Rubber* of Warren, Ohio. Coker's vintage tire line includes B.F. Goodrich, US Royal, Firestone and some Michelin. Coker also offers its own line of antique tires under **The Commander** and **Coker Classic** labels, which are a more affordable alternative to its major brand tires.

Coker believes that American antique cars not only deserve but require U.S.-built tires, and it prides itself on providing the best American-made tires whenever possible.

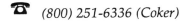 *(800) 251-6336 (Coker)*

# ★☆ 6 ☆★

# Stereo Equipment

## The Industry

America has long been one of the world's innovators in the design and production of stereo components. Such respected names as McIntosh, Harman Kardon and Acoustic Research originated in the United States. These companies and others produced many of the leading edge components of the 1950s and 1960s.

Although the U.S. lost most of the low-end stereo market in the 1970s, U.S. companies have remained at the forefront of mid- and higher-end components. In fact, the United States is widely regarded as a leader in the stereophonics industry.

Although Japanese companies produce a great deal of stereo equipment, it is generally low quality equipment. For example, *Sony*, one of the most commonly recognized names in the industry, produces speakers that dealers call "wretched."

One of the reasons Japanese quality trails behind is that Japanese companies are most noted for stereo rack systems. A rack system is a stereo with all the components put together, or "racked." Unwary customers have been attracted by the seeming convenience of rack systems, which save them the effort of purchasing the stereo components separately. Consumers have also been dazzled by the impressive—but often ineffectual—array of lights and other complicated-looking mechanisms found on rack systems. But dealers say "beware": Simpler is better in the world of stereophonics. And simple, quality-design, separately purchased speakers and amplifiers are areas where American manufacturers excel.

As with many products, "American-made" stereo components often contain some foreign-made parts. For example, American speakers usually contain woofers from Germany. With that qualification aside, many of the world's best stereo components are made right here in the U.S.

# Speakers

## Bose

Bose Corp. provides high quality at reasonable prices. Although some Bose speakers are imported, the majority are manufactured in Westborough, Mass. Bose (pronounced "bows") is famous for its development of the direct/reflective or omni-directional type of loudspeaker that floods a room with sound.

One of Bose's best products is the **Bose Lifestyle Music System** which is a complete music center including a CD player and AM/FM tuner. This system has no visible speakers, no bulky stacks of components or anything that resembles sound equipment. Bose's lifestyle system has gotten some excellent reviews. In a 1990 *New York Times* review Hans Fantel raved: "Hit the start button and suddenly the room fills with music of exemplary clarity and fullness."

Bose speakers are priced from $200 to $1,200 a pair. The Lifestyle system retails for a little under $2,000.

☎ *(800) 444-BOSE (Bose)*

## Cambridge SoundWorks

**Cambridge SoundWorks** is a brand new, red-hot company. Cambridge SoundWork's founder, Henry Kloss, was the designer of the original Acoustic Research and Advent speakers and co-founder of the Advent and KLH companies. Cambridge, his latest company, was founded just three years ago.

Cambridge is noted for some of the most reasonable speaker prices in the business. Reviewers found **The Ensemble**, Cambridge's first model, comparable to systems costing twice as much. With four speakers, two sub-woofers and two satellite speakers for mid-range and higher sounds, the Ensemble is a great deal.

Cambridge prices range from $75 for each mini speaker, to $749 for a transportable base case with amplifier. This system resembles a suitcase and can hide sub-woofers under furniture

Cambridge SoundWorks manufactures all of its speakers in Newton, Mass. Although Cambridge speakers are not available in stores, they can be ordered by calling their customer service number.

☎ *(800) AKA-HIFI (Cambridge SoundWorks)*

## Cerwin-Vega

**Cerwin-Vega** is a much-lauded company with a wide array of awards in the stereophonics industry. A repeated recipient of the Audio Engineers Society Award, Cerwin-Vega won an Academy Award for joining with Universal Studios to develop the "Sensurround" speaker for the 1970s thriller **Earthquake.** This speaker provided the most life-like sound that had ever been heard.

Cerwin-Vega's high-quality sound has earned it such patrons as the Pope and the Rolling Stones—thus the nickname "Voice of God" speakers. The pulse of the bass in Cerwin-Vega speakers is so strong that they are used in discos for the deaf.

The only family-owned company of its size, Cerwin-Vega was founded by the Czerwinski family 35 years ago in Simi Valley, Calif. Although the company has since built plants in Denmark and Canada, most of its products are made in Simi Valley.

Cerwin-Vega's speakers are moderately priced and can be found in major chain stores around the country.

## Dahlquist

**Dahlquist**, of Hauppage, N.Y., is a relatively new company. Founded in 1974, its red, white and blue boxes have become familiar items to stereo aficionados.

Dahlquist makes all of its speakers in Hauppage. They range from $600 to $2,000 a pair and can be found in a variety of retail stores including specialty and higher-priced chains.

## Infinity

**Infinity** speakers for home and car have won the company international fame. Critics have ranked the 23-year-old company's **IRS** (Industry Reference Standard) speakers as the most sonically accurate ever made.

Recently, Infinity improved upon the flagship IRS V with the **Modulus**. This new product derives its technology from the former speaker, but its size has been altered from 7 1/2 feet tall to 12 by 7 by 11 inches. The former speaker sells for $60,000, the latter $3,300. More moderately priced Infinity bookshelf speakers start at around $200.

*The Infinity Modulus Loudspeaker*

Almost all of Infinity's speakers are manufactured in its North Ridge, Calif., and Chatsworth, Calif., plants, although a few of its car speakers are produced overseas. Infinity products are sold at specialty stores nationwide.

☎ *(800) 765-5556 (Infinity)*

## International Jensen

**International Jensen** is another company favored by critics and public alike.

When Peter Jensen, a Danish immigrant, founded the company in 1927, he probably did not guess how successful it would become. The March 1988 issue of *Fortune* magazine included Jensen's **Advent** among the industry's Top 100 Made in the USA products.

Jensen was the first company to design and manufacture a car loudspeaker, and it was the first to use graphite in its speakers. Jensen also started a trend in the 1960s with its high quality two way design Advent speakers

International Jensen markets its products under the **Jensen, Phase Linear** and **Advent** labels. Speakers are priced from $199 to $1,000 a pair.

Although 90% of International Jensen's products are made in Punxstawnie, Pa, Cumberton and Clinton, N.C., Dallas, Texas, and Benicia, Calif., a few of its car stereos and CD players are imported.

*The "Graduate" loudspeaker from International Jensen's Advent label*

## Magnepan

**Magnepan**, manufacturer of the "Maggie" loudspeaker, started in 1968 in White Bear Lake, Minn., where the company still does all of its manufacturing. The Maggie is a form of ribbon speaker, also known as a dipole radiator. Invented in 1966, these two inch thick speakers resemble room dividers more than speakers because of their unusual look. An enormous hit when they reached the market in 1972, more than 100,000 Maggies were sold around the world— and Magnepan was firmly established as a company to contend with.

*Magnepan's "Maggie"*

Although their quality is recognized worldwide, Magnepans may not be the speakers for all listeners. Their subtlety is ideal for jazz or classical music, but the bass is not strong enough for many types of rock'n'roll.

## Polk Audio

Polk Audio, headquartered in Baltimore, Md., is another top-line U.S. speaker manufacturer. The company was started in 1972 in a garage by a group of friends from Johns Hopkins University. Polk soon flowered into what dealers claimed, in a 1988 *Inside Track* newsletter, to be the very best manufacturer in both home and car stereos. Polk speakers have won nearly every award in the industry, including the Audio Video Grand Prix awards every year for 13 years and several design/engineering awards at the Consumer Electronics Show.

Around 90% of Polk speakers are manufactured in the U.S. in the company's Baltimore factory.

# Amplifiers and Pre-amplifiers

## Audio Research

**Audio Research Corp.** is a manufacturer of top-end amps and pre-amps. Originally founded in Minneapolis, this company is a favorite of old music lovers. Audio Research was one of the first companies to make it possible to listen to old LPs again. Their **PHI** phono preamplifier recovers previously hidden nuances in black vinyl, so that old records sound even better than when they were new.

Audio Research's **LS1 Stereo Line Stage Amplifier** includes their famous hybrid tube/solid-state circuit technology. In 1992 Audio introduced the **LS2**, which includes all the technology of the LS1 plus balanced outputs—a growing trend in high-end audio. The LS2 has a minimalist design that makes this model more affordable. Ken Kessler declared in the *HI FI News and Record Review* of December 1991 that the LS2 is a "one-tube hybrid, line level pre-amp without a sonic fingerprint."

All Audio Research amplifiers are manufactured in Minneapolis, Minn. They range from $1,000 to $1,500 and can be found in independent audio specialty stores.

## Carver

**Carver Corp.** was founded in 1979 by Bob Carver, who also founded Phase Linear Corp., now owned by International Jensen. Carver is based in Lynnwood, Wash., where the company does its U.S. manufacturing.

Although approximately 60% of Carver products and virtually all of its hi-fi equipment are made overseas, the company continues to build all of its professional amplifiers and many of its mobile amplifiers and crossovers (for cars and boats) here.

## Counterpoint

Counterpoint Electronics, based in Vista, Calif., was the first company to manufacture a "phoneless" line control amplifier. Counterpoint products have won numerous awards, including the Hi-Fi Grand Prix Award and the Component of the Year Award. In 1991 Counterpoint won three major prizes in Japan, as well as the acclaimed Taiwanese Apollon ("highest recommended to buy") Prize.

In 1991 Counterpoint released its first all solid-state units: the **Solid 8 Line Level Preamp**, and the **Solid 1 Power Amplifier**. Both feature advanced FET/bipolar cascode technolgy and differential complementary circuit topology, which eliminates common solid state "grain colorations." Both are 19 inches wide.

☎ *(800) 275-2743 (Counterpoint)*

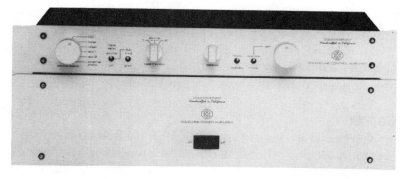

*A Counterpoint Solid 1 Power Amplifier*

Counterpoint has some of the highest quality products on the market, but also some of the most expensive.

Counterpoint's top of the line products sell for close to $8,000. Counterpoint designs and produces all of its products in Vista.

## McIntosh

**McIntosh Laboratory,** established in 1949 by Frank H. McIntosh, is the "grandfather" of all American stereo makers. All of its products are USA-made in Binghamton, N.Y.

Since its inception, McIntosh has designed and produced more than 150 different audio products. Its original product, the **Model 50WI amplifier,** received rave reviews. This amplifier earned the first of 34 patents awarded to McIntosh Laboratory. The **Unity Coupled 50W1 Power Amplifer** was the first amplifier that could truly be classifed as HI FI because harmonic and intermodulation distortion levels were less than 1% throughout the audio range of 10Hz to 20,000Hz.

Like Audio Research Corp., McIntosh has concentrated on components geared toward reproducing sound from old LPs—a comforting notion for old nostalgics.

McIntosh's products can be found nationwide in both major chain stores and private dealers.

# Compact Disc Players

## California Audio Labs

California Audio Labs is one of three American manufacturers that make high quality compact disc players. Its products are all made in Huntington Beach, Calif.

Cal Audio's **Icon** and **Tercet** models have terrific reputations in the stereophonic world. Of the two, the $700 Icon is the better choice. Although the Tercet costs twice as much as the Icon, its performance level is not much higher.

## McIntosh

While McIntosh is better known for its amplifiers, its compact disc players have attracted world renown. McIntosh's first CD player, the **Model MCD7007**, was introduced to the public in 1985. This CD player retails for just under $2,000.

*The McIntosh MCD7007 compact disc player*

Last year, McIntosh began producing a CD disc changer to complement its CD players. McIntosh's CD players and disc changers are made in the same Binghamton, N.Y. plant as its amplifiers and speakers.

## Theta

This company was founded five years ago by Mike Moffat in Van Nuys, Calif., and quickly developed one of the finest reputations in the industry.

**Theta** manufactures its only CD player—the **Theta Data** in Agora Hills, Calif. This excellent CD player costs $2,400, although an optional assortment of digital processors run an additional $1,250 - $5,000.

Theta products can be found in high-end audio stores across the nation.

# Telephones and Fax Machines

## The Industry

The U.S. telephone industry has dwindled down to three major manufacturerers: **AT&T**, **Comdial** and **Cortelco**.

Comdial, which specializes in business phones, and Cortelco, which makes phones for the home, do most of their manufacturing in the U.S. AT&T, which manufactures its home phones and most other AT&T products abroad, produces only a small percentage of high quality business phones in the U.S.

However, thanks to **Motorola**, the United States is very competitive in the cellular phone industry. Although Motorola is the single cellular phone manufacturer in the US, it controls one-quarter of the world's market, and makes cellular phone systems lauded by, among others, Japan's top manufacturers.

## Home and Business Phones

### Cortelco

Cortelco is the best source of American-made home telephones. Cortelco, which is headquartered in Memphis, Tenn., manufactures most of its products in Corinth, Minn., although the company does some manufacturing in Canada and Puerto Rico.

Cortelco is currently the **only** U.S. manufacturer of single-line consumer telephones. The **Trendline** phones, one of its most popular brands, includes, among other things, a memory of up to nine numbers, a call directory, and three-number emergency autodial. The cost is $44.95.

The **Citation** and **Tribute** series are also popular brands, costing $44.95 and $54.95. Both models come with user-friendly indented buttons and a comfortable, light handset. Advanced models of the phones include memory, last number redial and a directory.

Only a few Cortelco telephones are sold under the Cortelco name. Most are sold under the name brand **ITT** . This is because of Cortleco's initial association with ITT. Although Cortelco is currently an independent American corporation, the company continues to use the ITT label because it is one that consumers are already familiar with. In the coming years Cortelco will increase the number of telephones sold under its own name.

☎ *(601) 287-3771 (Cortelco)*

## AT&T

AT&T is a company whose name is practically synonymous with telephones and whose contributions to the telephone industry are immense. With this record, it is unfortunate that this American company manufactures comparatively little in the United States. However, the AT&T telephones that are manufactured in the States are among the best.

The **Merlin** system, manufactured in plants in Denver, Colo., and Shreveport, La., was a breakthrough in telephone technology. These office phone systems, which include conference calling, speaker functions, a timer, LED time and date displays, and a feature that identifies incoming callers, are widely used in offices across the United States.

There are three different models of Merlins: Merlin I, which has up to eight lines, Merlin II, which has 40, and the new Merlin Legend, which has 56 lines.

The **Partner** is another U.S.-made AT&T telephone. This new, popular office telephone is smaller and less complex than the Merlin, but has similar attributes and design.

☎ *(800) 628-2888 (AT&T)*

## Comdial

**Comdial Corp.** is the best source of American-made business phones. Originally based in California, this young company is now headquartered and manufactures in Charlottesville, Va. With 95% of the labor in a Comdial telephone from the Charlottesville plant (5% overseas) and 70% of the component parts coming from the U.S.—Comdial telephones are as American as you can get.

Comdial offers an extensive line of modestly priced business phones. The company's flagship product is the **Execu-Tech** business telephone system, which accounts for over 60% of the company's sales. ExecuTech systems include over 90 built-in features, such as simplified personal inter-office messaging, status of office phones at a glance, one-button intercom signaling and off-hook voice announce. The Execu-Tech also offers subdued or louder tone signals, depending on the urgency of the call, and "barge-in" calls.

*The ExecuTech 23-line Speakerphone (l) and Executive Hybrid (r)*

121

The ExecuTech is particularly efficient at outside calling. These phones are equipped with a stunning variety of outside call features, including group trunk access, which reduces the number of outside lines needed at any given station, and Station Message Detailed Recording to manage long-distance cost by line and station. In addition, there are flexible, any-number restrictions for both long distance and local calls, 10 to 30 programmable personal one-button auto-dial numbers, 50 additional systemwide speed dial numbers or access codes, last number and saved number redial, auto redial and optional background music.

☎ *(804) 978-2200 (Comdial)*

# Motorola Cellular and Cordless Telephones

## Cellular

The nine-year-old cellular phone industry is one in which American business is thriving. Although **Motorola** is the only company making cellular telephones in the U.S., it is one of the most powerful corporations in the industry and controls a quarter of the world market.

Most Motorola products are manufactured in its Arizona, Texas, Massachusetts, Illinois and Florida plants, although the company does produce in as many as 53 other countries. That most Motorola products are still manufactured in the U.S. is reflected in the fact that 60% of their employees are American and 40% live in other countries.

Motorola has revolutionized the industry in many ways. The company's ground-breaking **MicroTAC**, which weighed under one pound, was an enormous breakthrough in telephone technology. With the introduction of a telephone that customers could carry in their shirt pockets, Motorola not only changed the public's ideas about quick, convenient communication, but also changed the general attitude toward cellular phone technology. Says Robert N. Weisshappel, senior vice president and general manager of

Motorola's Pan American Cellular Subscriber Group: "People who were only mildly interested in cellular before were suddenly excited by the technology and particularly surprised and proud that an American company was at the forefront of a technological revolution."

*Motorola's brand- new "MicroTAC Lite"*

The MicroTAC won numerous product and product design awards from all over the world, including the Nikkei Award for a best new product of the year and the G-Mark design prize—both from Japan.

The company's latest product, the **MicroTAC Lite Digital Personal Communicator Telephone,** is the lightest and most advanced cellular telephone in the world. Weighing only 7.7 ounces and measuring 11.6 cubic inches, this remarkable phone follows in the steps of the original MicroTAC, which was the first functional telephone to weigh less than a pound. At less than half a pound, the new MicroTAC Lite is the world's lightest commercially available personal telephone.

Some of the MicroTAC Lite's features include a 911 override, which allows the user to make emergency calls even if the phone is locked, storage of up to 99 32-digit phone numbers, auto answer and a menu mode that allows the caller to view, select or clear features from a user-friendly list. This amazing cellular telephone comes complete with its own carrying case.

Motorola's **Tough Talk Transportable** fills another niche in the cellular market. Complete with carrying case, the Tough Talk weighs under 10 pounds and offers at least two full hours of fully transportable use before recharging is necessary.

The company also manufactures several cellular phones exclusively for automobiles. All of these phones have at least 100 number memory and can be equipped with the **D.V.S.P. II Digital Vehicular Speaker Phone.** The speaker is completely duplex in operation, which allows both parties to speak simultaneously without either being aware that a speaker phone is being employed.

Motorola's cellular phones are also sold under the **Pulsar, Sears' America Series** and **Montgomery-Ward's Ambassador II** labels.

## Cordless

While Motorola is especially known for its cellular phones, the company also makes cordless phones. The **America Series Secure Clear Cordless** line offers the convenience of a cordless telephone, with an almost impenetrable guard against eavesdropping. The security found in these phones is revolutionary in an age when a private conversation on a cordless phone is nearly impossible.

The **America Series 300** model features a one-hour battery back-up in case of power outage, 10 channels, a battery saver switch that extends the handset battery life for up to five weeks between charges, 65,000 randomly selected security codes to prevent unauthorized use of the owner's phone service, nine memories for speed dialing and the maximum power allowed by the FCC for highest range performance.

**The America Series 500** offers all the features of the 300 plus both a handset and base keypad, a speakerphone for hands-free operation and use of the phone when the handset is absent, an intercom and paging feature for three-way conversations, a visual channel indicator and a special button for emergency dialing.

☎ *(800) 247-4300 (Motorola)*

# Facsimile Machines

The world's first fax machine was invented by the American AT&T in the 1920s when it developed the technology to transmit wire service photographs.

Today's fax machine market is almost exclusively dominated by Japanese companies. In fact, there are no fax machines manufactured in the United States by American companies.

However, there are two American companies producing fax boards and one Japanese company assembling fax machines in the U.S.

## Canon

The Japanese **Canon** company assembles two fax machines in the United States. The **FAX-270S** is assembled in Canon's plant in Richmond, Va. This fax machine includes memory reception of up to 14 pages, memory transmission of up to 20 pages, 64 levels of gray scale half tones, an automatic document feeder of up to 30 sheets, automatic redialing and a confidential mailbox.

The **FAX-A501**, which is assembled partly in Richmond and partly in Japan, features "Super De-Curl," which takes out the annoying curl from fax-paper, and a "receiving restriction" that eliminates "junk faxes."

## Rockwell International

While it is disheartening to think of how few choices the Made in the USA consumer has to make in the facsimile machine industry, he or she can still see American influence when looking **inside** one of the machines. Even though there is not a single American manufacturer of fax machines, **Rockwell International**, an American company, supplies the majority of the computer modem boards found in fax machines.

With over 15 million units sold, Rockwell's **R96F** is the world's most popular modem board for use in facsimile machines. This small piece of equipment is the "brains" of a fax machine, allowing a machine to send and receive digital signals across phone lines. The rest of a fax machine is basically a telephone and printer packaged together.

Rockwell's modems are manufactured in labs in El Paso, Texas, and Newport Beach, Calif. This American company is highly respected both in the States and in Japan and has won both the prestigious American *Malcolm Baldrige Award* and medals from Japan's revered Sharp Corp. Rockwell modems are regarded equally highly elsewhere in the world. In fact, more than 70 percent of the world's fax machines contain Rockwell modems.

## Brooktrout Technology

This Massachusetts-based company produces circuit boards that enable personal computers to send and receive messages. Fax circuit boards are less expensive than stand-alone fax machines and have several other advantages. For example, incoming and outgoing messages can be stored in computer memory and documents can be printed on plain paper.

So before buying a foreign-made fax machine, consider buying a Brooktrout fax board for your computer instead. Most large mail-order computer supply companies sell these fax boards.

# ★☆ 8 ☆★
# The Home Office

## Introduction

This chapter suggests some of the top American-made personal computers, printers, laptops, word processors and copy machines suitable for home use. The chapter does not attempt to be comprehensive, but rather offers a few, highly select choices.

Consumers should note that all of these products contain at least some imported components and that in this particular chapter, "American-made" generally means the final assembly was done in the United States. This is a reflection of the overwhelming global nature of the computer industry.

## Personal Computers

### Datacomp

Datacomp is the best choice for those interested in a genuine American-made computer. **Datacomp Corp**. of McLean, Va., is the only U.S. computer manufacturer that is firmly committed to producing an all-union family of computers made from American-produced components. In fact, Datacomp computers contain 90% U.S. components—the highest percentage of any American-made computer.

As company President Clay Kime explains, "We have a sincere belief in America's leadership in both workmanship and technology. Despite trade policies and tax laws which stack the decks against American-based producers and

American workers, we intend to hold to the integrity of our product."

Datacomp supplies computers to the U.S. government, including the Navy, unions and businesses across the country.

To date, Datacomp computers have been exclusively designed for the business setting. However, this year Datacomp will introduce the **DCC 386/SX**—its first computer designed and priced for individual use.

Datacomp computers are 100% compatible—they run all industry standard software programs—and are backed by a national on-site service network.

Datacomp computers must be directly ordered from the company.

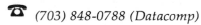 *(703) 848-0788 (Datacomp)*

*The New Datacomp DCC 386/SX*

## Tandy

**Tandy Corp.**, which is the parent company of Radio Shack, produces all of its desktop computers in Fort Worth, Texas. Most Tandy laptops are also produced in Fort Worth. This U.S. company probably has a higher percentage of U.S. content than many of its fellow U.S. computer companies because Tandy has its own injection molding, current board and wire and cable manufacturing facilities in the U.S.

The best Radio Shack desktops for home use are the **1000 RL** and the **1000 RLX**. The more advanced **2500 SX** is well-suited for either home or office and includes the impressive **2500 SX Multimedia model,** which features a CD-ROM drive and an advanced audio board for multimedia applications. Tandy computers can be purchased at Radio Shack stores and dealers across the nation.

*Tandy computers*

# What About IBM and Apple?

## IBM

**International Business Machines** is the grand-daddy of computers. IBM is an American company that started out in the early 1900s as a manufacturer of clocks and other mechanical devices. By the 1950s, IBM was producing some of the world's first computers. Today, IBM is a massive, global company that manufactures its computers and components all over the world. Like many global companies, IBM assembles its products in the markets they will be sold in. Consequently, all IBM computers sold in the United States are assembled in Raleigh, N.C., or Austin, Texas.

IBM's **PS-1** (Personal System 1) series is an ideal choice for home personal computer needs. These entry level computers are available in a variety of preloaded packages that include display terminal and keyboard. All models retail for under $2,500, with some models available for as little as $1,000. PS-1 computers can be found at IBM dealers and Sears stores nationwide.

IBM's **PS-2** series offers computers that are a step above the PS-1 models in terms of applications, storage/memory and upgradability. PS-2 models, which are designed for a variety of business needs, are advanced enough to take on peripherals and

*An IBM 386 SX home computer*

132

additional storage bays and run large-memory software programs such as Lotus. There are 14 PS-2 models to choose from—depending on your business needs and budget. One model to examine carefully is the best-selling **PS-2 model 55 SX**, which retails for just under $3,000 and is found in offices across the nation.

## Apple

Like IBM, Apple is an American company that has become very much of a global player. The first Apple computer was created in a California garage in the 1970s. Since this backyard start, Apple computers have played a large part in pushing the industry toward offering moderately priced, user-friendly computers for personal use. Like most computer companies today, Apple manufactures its computer components both in and out of the United States. The company also splits its final assembly operations between the U.S. and countries like Singapore and Ireland.

In general, Apple imports its basic, most affordable computers into the U.S. For example, Apple's basic Macintosh Classic computers are manufactured out of the U.S. So are its Macintosh LC models. Both of these computer lines sell for $1,000-$2,500 and are unfortunately the Apple computers that would be most suited for home use.

However, if you are willing to spend extra, Apple's top of the line **Macintosh II** computers are assembled in the United States. These computers are available in the IIsi, IIci and IIfx lines—each one a bit more advanced (and more expensive) than the next. Macintosh IIs range from around $3,769 suggested retail for the least expensive IIsi model to over $8000 for the top-of-the line IIfx model. Apple's premium **Macintosh Quadra** line ($5,600 - $9,000) is also assembled in the United States. As for Apple's newest product, the **Powerbook Notebook Computer**—some of these are assembled in the U.S. and some are not, so be careful.

# Printers

American computer companies assemble a wide range of printers in the United States. However, the only laser printers currently designed, developed and manufactured in the United States are those made by **Lexmark**, an alliance company of IBM.

Lexmark-made laser printers, which are sold under the IBM label, offer laser quality for both home and larger business needs. Lexmark's new **IBM LaserPrinter 4029 series** is an exciting line of printers that can be used with either IBM or Apple PCs and offer greatly improved speed and print quality. This series, which ranges from single-use models to high performance LAN capability printers, recently received *P.C. Magazine*'s technical excellence award.

The ideal 4029 series printer for the home is the **IBM LP-5E**. This printer gives home or small business printing needs 300 x 300dpi laser quality for $1,595 and under. The Laser-Printer 5E comes with a Motorola 10MHz controller and a high-speed parallel/serial interface for faster processing and prints five pages a minute.

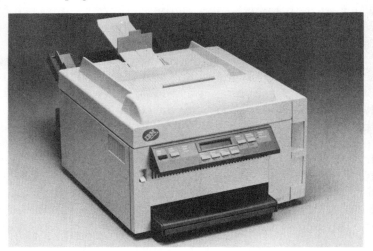

*The IBM LaserPrinter 4029-5E*

# Laptop Computers

The laptop segment is the fastest growing part of the personal computer market. There are a plethora of laptops on the American market—many of these are made in the U.S., many are not. Some of the best all-American laptops are manufactured by **AVG Advanced Technologies.**

AVG has been a leader and innovator in industrial controls and computer components for over 15 years. Although this privately held U.S. company has supplied laptop companies with circuit boards (the major component of a laptop) for years, it wasn't until 1990 that AVG introducd its own laptop.

Two years later, AVG offers eight different laptop models. All of them—from casings to current boards—are 100% made in the U.S.A. in Philadelphia, Pa., and Chicago, Ill.

*The AVG 386SX laptop*

The **AVG 386SX** weighs 13 pounds, and, among other features, includes 2MB or 4MB dynamic RAM memory, 1.44 MB floppy and 40-535 MB shock-mounted hard disk drive, MS-DOS software compatibility and a built-in charger.

This state-of-the-art laptop is not only moderately priced, but designed for complete dependability. The 386SX has shock-mounted disk drives and impact resistant polycarbonate casings for extreme durability. To further ensure reliability, each unit is subjected to rigorous quality control testing, including a rigorous 110° F burn-in period.

☎ *(800) LAP-AVG1 (AVG)*

# Smith Corona Typewriters and Word Processors

**Smith Corona Corp.**, based in New Canaan, Conn., entered the typewriter business more than 100 years ago. Today, Smith Corona is the world's largest manufacturer of portable electric typewriters and personal word processors. It is also the only American manufacturer of portable electronic typewriters and personal word processors. Most Smith Corona typewriters and personal word processors are manufactured in the United States in Cortland, N.Y.

## Personal Word Processors

Smith Corona offers an extensive line of personal word processors, or PWPs. Every word processor in the Smith Corona line comes with a standard 3.5-inch drive that provides permanent storage and enables users to easily transfer information between PWPs and personal computers.

Most of Smith Corona's PWPs are MS-DOS compatible, with an ASCII translator for personal computer-PWP transfers and WordPerfect® converter software. For ease of use, most PWP models feature a Graphical User Interface that allows the user to "see what they get." High-end models have an optional fax / modem card that snaps right onto the PWP, allowing the user to exchange information between compatible PWPs, personal computers and Group III fax machines worldwide.

Smith Corona's newest personal word processor is model **PWP 3800**, which is ideal for the home or office. This model features a 12-inch CRT amber monitor for clear text viewing, built-in word processing software, a daisy wheel printer and standard 3.5-inch disk drive and MS-DOS capability.

*The Smith Corona Personal Word Processor model 3200*

## Portable Electronic Typewriters

Smith Corona also offers five models of portable electronic typewriters that are designed for either home or office work. Most of these "typewriters" have advanced text and word processing features. The entry-level **XL 1800** is a portable, easy-to-use typewriter that is ideal for students or home use. The affordable XL 1800 ($150) includes automatic functions such as bold print, decimal tab and full line correction. It is also equipped with the company's patented Correcting Cassette, which makes correcting mistakes a breeze.

The **XL 2800** is a full-featured electronic typewriter that includes a 75,000 word Spell-Right® dictionary and a Word-Find® feature. The **XD 4800** and **XD 5800** models are word processing typewriters, which feature memory, word processing functions and, in the case of the 5800, a 24-character liquid crystal display.

*Smith Corona XD 7800 word processing typewriter*

The top of the line Smith Corona "typewriter" is the **XD 7800**. This word processing typewriter features a two-line, 40-character liquid crystal display and 20,000 characters of editable memory that allows the typist to store, edit, recall and print text from memory. This machine is ideal for business and even has a Forms Layout feature that allows the typist to quickly type pre-printed forms.

# Personal Copiers

There are few American-made desktop copiers. The vast majority of this type of copier are assembled overseas. However, **Xerox Corp.** the inventor of the copy machine and the best name in the business, still assembles one desktop copier in the U.S. The **Xerox 5011** desktop copier, which is assembled in Webster, N.Y., sells for approximately $2,895.

*The Xerox 5011 R/E Convenience Copier*

# ★☆ 9 ☆★
# Small Home Appliances

## The Industry

The U.S. undoubtedly uses more appliances than any other nation on earth. Americans seem to continually demand new and more innovative appliances. Consequently, American appliances are some of the best and most progressive in the world.

This chapter focuses on six small home appliances: toasters, blenders, food processors, coffee makers, microwave ovens and vacuum cleaners. While recommending specific American-made models that reflect a company's best products, the chapter also attempts to provide the consumer with a sense of the overall import/export production patterns of each company. Since almost every company mentioned imports some portion of its appliances, the overall production information should give the consumer some guidance in shopping beyond the recommended models. When in doubt, do not hesitate to turn over an appliance to read the country of origin marked on its bottom.

Although this section does not include large appliances, it should be noted that large appliances are no longer all American-made. Many U.S.-made large appliances contain an increasing number of imported parts, and some U.S. companies, particularly General Electric, do some final assembly in Mexico. The 1993 edition of 'Made in the U.S.A.' will include an in-depth discussion of large American-made appliances.

# Toasters

## Black & Decker

Although Black & Decker toasters are almost entirely imported, all Black & Decker **Toast-R-Oven®** broilers and toaster ovens are made in the U.S. Black & Decker's top-of-the-line toaster oven is the **Ultra Oven Toast-R-Oven® Broiler** ($100.98) which not only toasts, but broils, bakes and defrosts. This oven has an eight-slice capacity, a continuously cleaning interior, and a bell that signals when toast is ready.

## Proctor-Silex

Although in recent years this company has shifted a large amount of production to Mexico, the Proctor-Silex/Hamilton Beach company still manufactures many of its small appliances in the U.S.—including the world's largest line of toasters and toaster ovens.

One of Proctor-Silex's newest toasters is the **Lot-A-Slot Coolwall Toaster** (model T2830; 46.95), which features a cool-to-the-touch exterior and an easy cleaning crumb tray. This toaster's interior bread slots will also position all bread widths, including difficult-to-toast bagels and muffins. Lot-A-Slot's sleek, elongated design is quite distinctive and saves a great deal of counter space.

*Proctor-Silex Lot-A-Slot Coolwall Toaster*

## Sunbeam

Sunbeam/Oster makes about 80 percent of its appliances in the United States. Sunbeam's line of two and four slice toasters includes one of the most interesting toasters on the market. The **Model 20030**, introduced in 1945, is believed to be the oldest toaster in continuous production. Today's Model 20030, which retails for $79, combines a timeless art deco exterior with the best of modern technology. It is a fully automatic, self-lowering toaster with a radiant console feature that "senses" the amount of moisture in the bread and gives it a uniform toast.

## Toastmaster

Toastmaster manufactures approximately 90% of its small appliances and every single one of its extensive line of toasters and toaster ovens in the United States. Toastmaster's **Cool Steel Toasters®** feature extra wide slots and a cool-touch metal exterior that does not get as hot as a traditional steel toasters.

*Toastmaster "Cool Steel" two-slice wide slot toaster*

# Blenders

## Hamilton Beach

Proctor-Silex/Hamilton Beach manufactures all of its Hamilton Beach blenders in the United States. The 1992 line features styling updates as well as the addition of pulse-speed and blend and serve container options. One of Hamilton Beach's most noteworthy blenders is the ultra versatile **Blendmaster Blender Center**. For $69.99, this blender set includes a 44 oz. basic jar, three different sizes of blend-serve-store plastic jars and a 32oz. stainless steel jar for blender drinks such as frozen marguaritas. The Blender Center also features ultra modern "eurostyling" with white and teal graphics and 14 different speeds.

## Oster

Although Sunbeam/Oster manufactures roughly 80% of its home appliances in the U.S., Oster blenders are all made here. Of special note is the model 85208, the **Oster Blender with Glass Container**. This basic white "Osterizer" features a high quality glass container, 12 different blending speeds, an all-metal drive system and a $54 price tag.

# Food Processors

## Hamilton Beach

All of the Hamilton Beach food processors are made in the U.S.A., including the new **702R** ($49.99), which features an easy access rocker switch, two-speed processing for a variety of applications from mincing and shredding to mixing salad dressings, and the latest in Hamilton Beach styling.

## Oster

Most of Oster's line of Kitchen Center food processors are made in the U.S., although a few models are assembled in Mexico from U.S.-made components. The touch tone "**5-in-1" Kitchen Center** is a remarkable, versatile appliance that is well worth its $250 price tag. This remarkable 16-speed machine can perform an endless variety of tasks. It is a blender, stand mixer, doughmaker, slicer/shredder and food processor—all in one central unit. The 5-in-1 Kitchen

Center set includes two large mixing bowls and a 250-page recipe booklet. Other attachments can be bought separately, including a juicer and an icecream maker.

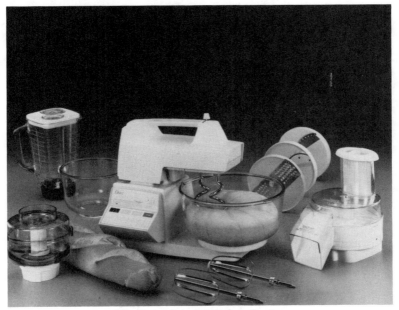

*The Oster 5-in-1 Kitchen Center*

## Regal

Regal makes 95% of its appliances including its 10 models of food processors in Jacksonville, Ark., and Kewaskum, Wis. The **Regal Electronic Food Processor** (model K663BK; $132.90) is a versatile food processor that is capable of many of the same functions as more expensive processors—including everything from beating eggs to kneading dough. This processor features a direct drive motor that eliminates problems with stretched and broken belts. It also has a special safety feature—the machine will not operate unless the lid is securely in place. Regal's latest processor is the economical 72 oz. **Regal Food Processor** (K7755), which retails for $78.95.

Regal also manufactures the famous **La Machine** food processors.

*The economical Regal Food Processor*

# Coffeemakers

### Black & Decker

Black & Decker is one of the leading designers of coffeemakers—almost all of which are made in the U.S. (imported models tend to be the smallest capacity Black & Decker coffeemakers). Some of Black & Decker's best coffeemakers are the models that brew coffee directly into a thermal carafe, which keeps it warm for up to eight hours. The carafe's attractive molded plastic outer body allows it to double as an attractive beverage server for either hot or cold beverages.

Black & Decker's **Thermal Carafe Drip Coffee Maker** ($79.98) features an analog clock/timer that can be set at night, so morning coffee is ready when you are, and an automatic shut-off safety function. Black & Decker also offers two models of **Spacemaker Plus** thermal carafe coffeemakers which are installed under cabinets to maximize counter space without sacrificing full capacity.

Thermal Carafe and Spacemaker coffeemakers aside, Black & Decker offers a large variety of American-made 10- and 12-cup capacity drip coffeemakers. The **DCM900** drip coffeemaker is a moderately priced ($25.98) compact, ultra-contemporary design 10-cup coffeemaker that takes up very little counter space and looks great in any kitchen. The DCM900 includes a hot plate that automatically turns off after the coffee has finished brewing, a simple on/off switch and an "on" light that reminds you the coffeemaker is on.

## Regal

Regal makes Polyperk percolator coffeepots as well as drip coffeemakers. Regal's 12-cup drip coffeemaker with a digital clock, model **K7586**, sells for $50. One of Regal's best values in coffeemakers is the model **K700**. This new coffeemaker is a sleek, compact, contemporary design 10-cup coffeemaker that features quick, quiet brewing and a thermostatically controlled warming plate—all for $26.95.

*The Black & Decker Thermal Drip Coffeemaker (l) and the value-engineered Regal 7600 Coffeemaker (r)*

## Mr. Coffee

Although Mr. Coffee is a famous name in American cof-feemakers, this company imports about half of its cof-feemakers. However, one of the company's newest coffeemaker lines, **The Accel**, will initially be exclusively produced in the U.S.

# Microwave Ovens

The age of the microwave oven has changed cooking habits across the country. Although microwave technology was invented by Raytheon Corp. in the U.S. in the 1940s, most of the microwaves sold in the U.S. today are imports. Today, there are only three companies manufacturing American-made microwaves.

### Frigidaire

The Frigidaire Co. (formerly White Consolidated In-dustries) manufactures almost all of its microwave ovens for its **Frigidaire** and **Tappan** labels in Dalton, Ga. The only imported Frigidaire and Tappan microwaves are the small subcompact models (.4 and .6 cu. ft.) which will be phased out in '92, and its over-the-range models. All of its larger countertop models (.8, 1.0 and 1.3 cu. ft.), which comprise over 95% of the company's business, are made in Dalton.

One of Frigidaire's best offerings is the Tappan Speed-wave 1000, which is the only 1,000 watt counter top microwave on the

*Tappan's "Speedwave 1000" microwave oven*

market. This oven, which cooks approximately 25% faster than a standard 600-700 watt oven, is available in .8 and 1.3 cu. ft. sizes for $199 to $269.

## Amana

As was noted above, the microwave was invented in the U.S. by Raytheon in the 1940s. At first, Raytheon's microwave technology was used only in large institutional ovens. However, in 1965, Raytheon purchased the Amana Refrigeration Co., to help transform its revolutionary microwave technology into small ovens for home use.

Today, Amana still produces the majority of its top-quality **Amana** microwaves here in the U.S. in Amana, Iowa. Amana's imported models are its smaller ovens that measure less than a cubic foot (.6 or .8 cu. ft.). This year, Amana will introduce the American-made **RW322T** oven, which features cooking pads preprogrammed with the correct cooking times for a variety of items from mini meals to potatoes.

*Amana microwave oven model RW332T*

## Magic Chef

Magic chef is a division of **Maytag Corp**. With the exception of its over-the-range models, all **Magic Chef** microwaves are made in the U.S. in Anniston, Ala. Magic Chef microwaves are available in 15 different models ranging from its smallest .6 cu. ft. ovens to the largest 1.5 cu. ft. models.

# Vacuum Cleaners

## Black & Decker

It has been over 10 years since Black & Decker introduced the revolutionary Dustbuster cordless hand-held vacuum cleaner. From the everyday **Dustbuster** and **Dustbuster Plus** models to the more powerful **Dustbuster PowerPro** models, contemporary Dustbusters are still America's favorite hand-held cordless vacuum—and are still made in the U.S.A.

The PowerPro **DB2000** ($56.98) extra capacity model quickly picks up any mess—wet, dry and soggy—and has a special squeegee attachment that allows it to tackle messes on hard surfaces. The Powerpro **DB6000** heavy duty cordless vac is Black & Decker's best performing hand vacuum. This Dustbuster has two power settings, an optional Power Brush and a high performance motor that makes it ideal for any type of dry pickup. This model retails for approximately $72.

In addition to its cordless hand cleaners, Black & Decker also offers upright cordless vacuums, including the American-made **Dustbuster Upright Power Brush**, which is perfect for room-at-a-time cleanups. All Dustbuster cordless vacuums come with a handy storage unit that also serves as a recharger.

*The Black & Decker Heavy Duty PowerPro Dustbuster*

# Electrolux

The Electolux company of Marietta, Ga., has a reputation for making the highest quality vacuums in the world. All **Electrolux** vacuums sold in the U.S. are made in Bristol, Va. However, all vacuum cleaners sold under the name A.B. Electrolux (mostly found in Europe) are made by Electrolux's European sister company. Electrolux vacuums start at about $300 for an upright model, but are designed to last for 20 years.

# Eureka

The Eureka company manufactures virtually all of its vacuums in the U.S. in El Paso, Texas and Bloomington-Normal, Ill. Its only imports are a few hand-held vacuums and its "stick" brooms.

The newest of Eureka's 150 U.S.-made vacuums is its **Bravo** line. These upright vacuums feature on-board attachments and a hose that plugs into the top of the vacuum for cleaning drapes, furniture, etc. Although the Bravo line was just introduced this year, Eureka already has hundreds of thousands of orders for this new versatile vacuum cleaner. There are 10 different Bravo models all moderately priced at between $99 and $139.

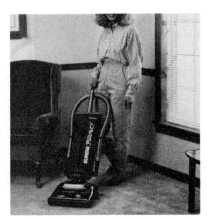

*The "Bravo Boss" by Eureka*

## Hoover

For many, the name Hoover is practically synonymous with the vacuum. Hoover has been manufacturing vacuums in North Canton, Ohio, since 1908. Today, 80% of Hoover full-sized vacuum cleaners are manufactured in the U.S., with the remaining 20% assembled in Mexico from U.S. parts.

Hoover leads the vacuum industry in upright cleaners that convert into cannister vacuums. Although Hoover invented a convertible vacuum cleaner back in the 1920s and even patented this attached tool vacuum in 1936, there wasn't any interest in this innovation until this decade.

Hoover's new **PowerMax** vacuum cleaners are top of the line dual use vacuum cleaners that feature automatic tool conversion. That is, the hose used for cannister type vacuuming is already attached to the vacuum. To switch from upright vacuuming to hose vacuuming for walls, ceilings and furniture, the user simply attaches one of the many on-board tools. The four PowerMax models are also self-propelled and "glide" across the carpet without being pushed. Hoover's PowerMax vacuums retail for between $349 and $449.

Hoover's **Elite II** vacuum cleaners are more modestly priced and offer something for every pocketbook. Like the PowerMax models, this extensive line of upright cleaners also features on-board tools and can easily be converted for cannister/hose vacuuming. However, on Elite II vacuums, the hose for cannister vacuuming must be manually attached.

*The Hoover PowerMax*

All PowerMax and Elite II vacuums are manufactured in North Canton, Ohio.

## Oreck

Oreck has been making commercial vacuum cleaners for over 25 years. A few years ago, the company introduced its first home use vacuum, the **Oreck XL**. Today, the Oreck XL line includes a variety of durable vacuums, including the **Hypoallergenic** line featuring double-wall outer bag, double inner bag vacuums, which retain 97% of the dust they take in. All Oreck vacuums are made in the U.S. and are designed for the long run.

# Miscellaneous Appliances

### Chef's Choice® Knife Sharpeners

Chef's Choice® knife sharpeners have won national and global acclaim. These revolutionary sharpeners are made in Avondale, Pa., and exported to department, cutlery and specialty stores in every major country—including Harrods of London and Tokyo's Mitsukoshi.

*Chef's Choice® Diamond Hone Sharpener*

By using a set of strong magnets to hold the knife "just so" and a diamond to sharpen, these machines turn out perfectly sharpened, perfectly honed knives—every time. The three-stage model that gives knives a state-of-the-art triple-bevel edge sells for around $80. The two-stage sharpener can be had for about $50. **Edgecraft Corp**. also offers a ScissorPro® scissor sharpener.

### Regal Griddles/Electric Grills

Regal manufactures a complete line of griddles and individual electric grills in the U.S.

### Swing-A-Way Can Openers

There are dozens of imported can openers on the market. However, many contend that Swing-A-Way manual can openers, which have been manufactured in St. Louis, Mo., for more than 50 years, perform better than any electric can opener.

# Ceiling Fans

Imported ceiling fans are often of inferior quality and can actually be dangerous. A few years ago, the U.S. Consumer Product Safety Commission recalled several models of cheap imported fans because their ceiling fixtures were not adequate to hold the fan. American-made ceiling fans are much better fans with high quality, long lasting motors and strong fixtures that keep the fan safely in place. Some of the best American-made ceiling fans are made by the following companies:

### Casablanca

**Casablanca Fan Co.** has been making high- quality ceiling fans in Pasadena, Calif., since 1973.

## Emerson

**Emerson** manufactures all of its ceiling fans in the U.S. in Hazelwood, Mo. Please note that this company is not affiliated with either Emerson Electronics or Emerson Radio.

## Fasco

This new company makes all of its ceiling fans in the U.S.

## Hunter

**Hunter** manufactures its top-of-the-line fans in the U.S., but imports its less expensive models from Taiwan.

# ★☆ 10 ☆★
# Sporting Goods

From playing in impromptu neighborhood games to cheering on the local high school or professional team—Americans love sports. Americans also like to keep fit. Since the fitness boom of the 1970s, Americans exercise more than ever before—and in every imaginable way. Americans jog, swim, lift weights, play organized team sports, rollerskate and just about anything else you can think of. Some people even call Americans sports or fitness "fanatics." It is no surprise, then, that U.S. manufacturers often lead the field in sports and fitness equipment.

## Personal Exercise Equipment

### Nautilus

**Nautilus** was one of the early pioneers in high quality personal exercise equipment. Although a number of companies produce such equipment today, Nautilus equipment is still widely considered the cream of the crop.

A Nautilus workout is designed to work all parts of the body to maintain and improve a full range of muscular motion. Although home Nautilus machines have been gradually phased out, Nautilus equipment is standard in many of the nation's best health clubs. All Nautilus equipment is manufactured in Independence, Va., and is exported virtually everywhere, including Europe, the Middle East, Asia and Australia.

☎ *(800) 874-8941 (Nautilus)*

## DP

**Diversified Products** , which manufactures all of its fitness equipment in Opelika, Ala., is one of the world's largest manufacturers of physical fitness equipment. From basic bench presses to benches equipped with arm and leg accessories, DP offers affordable equipment for a basic home weight workout.

DP also manufactures a number of high quality exercise bikes and treadmills for aerobic workouts. The gem of this product line is the **AirGometer,** which features dual action handlebars to combine an upper and lower body workout. The AirGometer's no impact workout is based on the principle that air resistance provides excellent cardiovascular conditioning.

DP also manufactures higher-end **Wynmor** fitness equipment for health clubs.

☎ *(800) 633-5730 (DP)*

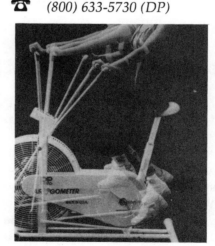

*Top of the line DP AirGometer*

## Soloflex

**Soloflex** is a home fitness machine that provides a tension workout based on rubber straps that simulate real weights. The Soloflex machine works a wide range of muscles and allows the user to exercise without straining muscles by attempting to lift too much.

One of the key advantages of the Soloflex is its versatility. The Soloflex can perform a range of exercises, including bench presses, squats and curls and dips. Another advantage of a Soloflex machine is its compactness. This personal fitness machine can fit in an area as little as four square feet.

All Soloflex machines are manufactured in Hillsboro, Ore., and are exported worldwide.

☎  *(800) 547-8802 (Soloflex)*

## NordicTrack

NordicTrack fitness machines simulate cross country skiing. In addition to exercising all of the body's major muscle groups, Nordic-Track also develops cardiovascular fitness. A Nordic-Track workout is easy on the knees and back, burns more calories than rowing machines or exercise bikes and is a great deal of fun.

All NordicTrack machines are manufactured in Chaska, Minn.

*NordicTrack*

☎  *(800) 328-5888 (NordicTrack)*

# Swim Accessories

## Tyr Swimsuits

All **Tyr** swimsuits sold in the U.S are made in Summit, Mich. The company offers close-fitting racing style suits as well as baggy, noncompetitive casual suits for men and a variety of women's one-piece suits. Tyr suits can be found at Herman's and other sporting goods shops nationwide.

## Hind Goggles

**Hind-Wells** manufactures every pair of its world renowned racing goggles in San Luis Obispo, Calif. Hind goggles have been worn by more record breaking competitive swimmers than any other goggle. They are comfortable, watertight goggles that provide excellent peripheral vision. The streamlined design also reduces water drag.

*A Tyr swimstuit*

☎ *(800) 426-4463 (Hind-Wells)*

## Barracuda Goggles

These award-winning goggles are made in Portland, Ore.

☎ *(800) 547-8664 (Barracuda)*

## A note on *Speedo*....

Speedo is perhaps the best known swimwear and swim accessories company in the United States. However, all Speedo swimsuits are manufactured in the Orient and Speedo goggles are made in Canada, Mexico and Taiwan.

## O'Brien Watersports Equipment

If you prefer to be on the water instead of swimming in it, O'Brien manufactures a range of watersports equipment in Redmond, Wash. Among other things, O'Brien offers top-quality water skis, inflatable tubes and ski vests.

# Baseballs

Although baseball was invented in the United States, there are no longer any baseballs made in the U.S. All of the large companies, including Wilson, Rawlings and Spalding, which claims to be "America's First Baseball Company," produce their baseballs in Haiti.

# Baseball Gloves

Finding a baseball glove made in the USA is almost as difficult as finding a baseball. There are only two major American manufacturers that still make baseball gloves in the U.S.

## Nokona

Nokona manufactures 100% of its baseball gloves in, you guessed it, Nokona, Texas. Although "Nokona" sounds foreign, this American company is named after a Comanche Indian chief and is firmly committed to making its products in the U.S. In fact, the Nokona slogan is, "Nokona is as American as baseball."

Nokona offers a full range of baseball and softball gloves, including a kangaroo hide glove made from Australian kangaroo hide. Nokona gloves sell for between $100 and $150.

Nokona also manufactures a complete line of both football and baseball protective equipment.

*A Nokona BM-76 baseball glove*

☎ *(800) 433-0957 (Nokona)*

## Rawlings

**Rawlings** makes about half of its gloves in the United States in Ava, Mo. The quickest way to determine if a Rawlings glove is made in the U.S. is to examine the stamp on the glove.

One of Rawlings' U.S.-made models is the top-of-the-line **Gold Glove**. These gloves are made from "Heart of the Hide" leather, which comes from the choicest five percent of American steers and undergoes an exclusive, expensive tanning process. The result is a top-notch, extremely durable glove that is favored by many of the nation's major league players.

☎ *(800) 729-5464 (Rawlings)*

# Baseball Bats

## Louisville Sluggers

The original **Louisville Slugger** was developed by baseball legends Pete "The Gladiator" Browning and "Bud" Hillerich in 1884 in Louisville, Ky. The pair created the bat to help Browning get out of a batting slump. The first time

Browning used the bat, he broke his slump with three hits and started the Louisville Slugger on the road to becoming a baseball tradition.

Today, **Hillerich and Bradsby Co.** manufactures 100% of its bats in the United States. The company offers aluminum bats that are manufactured in California and Kentucky, state-of-the-art Tennessee-made graphite bats and a range of wooden bats, crafted from mostly white ash in Indiana, New York and Pennsylvania.

☎ *(800) 282-2287 (Hillerich and Bradsby)*

*The new graphite "Louisville Slugger" baseball bat*

## Easton

**Easton Sports** specializes in aluminum and ceramic bats—made in Van Nuys, Calif. From the **Black Magic** to the **Ultra Light**, Easton makes bats for all levels of competition except professional. In fact, at the 1988 Olympics in Seoul, Team USA used Easton bats exclusively, as did 80 percent of their competitors.

One of Easton's newest bats is made from a composite of fiberglass, graphite and ceramic. At $125 and up, this state-of-the-art bat is aimed at the serious competitor.

# Basketball Equipment

## Basketballs

Like baseball, basketball is a sport that is native to the United States. However the only basketballs currently manufactured in the U.S. are special-order balls Wilson makes for the government. Even more disappointing is the fact that the official NBA basketball by Spalding is made in South Korea.

## Schutt

**Schutt Manufacturing Co.** makes all of its basketball rims and basketball rebounders in Litchfield and Knoxville, Tenn. Schutt's excellent glass and aluminum indoor and outdoor backboards are made by its Michigan supplier.

## Huffy

**Huffy** backboards, which are made by Huffy Sports in Chicago, Ill., are the only backboards that carry an NBA endorsement. Huffy's newest, most innovative backboards use the latest in composite construction and modern graphics as well as a unique elevator pole system.

☎ *(800) 558-5234 (Huffy)*

# Football Equipment

## Wilson

The all-American **Wilson** company produces all of its sports equipment in the U.S., including tennis balls, golf equipment, uniforms...and the **Official NFL Football**. In fact, Wilson's Ada, Ohio manufactured footballs have been used in every Super Bowl and NFL regular season game since 1941.

*A Wilson employee works on an official NFL football in Ohio*

# Gerry Cosby

**Gerry Cosby Co.** manufactures top quality shoulder pads in Sheffield, MA. Cosby shoulder pads ("The Professional's Choice") are the pads used by more than 350 of the players in the NFL, including Los Angeles Raiders star running back Roger Craig and all-pro linebacker Lawrence Taylor of the New York Giants.

Cosby pads are sized for players of all ages. The company also makes an excellent line of American-made equipment bags.

☎ *(800) 548-4003 (Gerry Cosby)*

# Golf Equipment

Although the game of golf originated in the British Isles, it is now a well-established, much-loved American sport. Nearly all types of golf equipment, including clubs, balls and shoes are made in the USA. U.S. golf equipment is exported to countries all over the world, including Japan where American-made golf equipment has become a status symbol. Some of the top names in *American-made* golf equipment are:

## U.S. Companies

**Lynx**—*(clubs), 100% U.S.-made, City of Industry, Calif.*
**Ping**—*(clubs, bags, balls), 100% U.S.-made, Phoenix, Ariz.*
**Taylor**—*(clubs), 100% U.S.-made, Calif., N.C., Tenn.*
**Wilson**— *(clubs, balls, and bags), 100% U.S.-made, Tenn.*
**Titleist**—*(clubs, balls), 100% U.S.-made, Mass., Calif.*
**Spalding**— *(balls), 100% U.S.-made in Chicopee, Mass.*
**Hillary and Bradsby**—*(clubs), 100% made in Jeffersonille, Ind.*

## Foreign companies

**Etonic** (Sweden)—*(shoes), 50% U.S.-made, Richmond, Minn.*
**McGregor** (Finland)—*(clubs), 100% assembled in Albany, Ga.*

# Tennis Equipment

## Rackets

Not a single tennis racket is manufactured in the United States. The last company to make rackets here was Head.

## Balls

Both **Wilson** and **Penn** make all of their tennis balls in the U.S., in Faltinon, S.C. and Phoenix, Ariz., respectively.

# Skating/Hockey Equipment

## Christian

**Christian** hockey sticks are made in Waroad, Minn., and exported all over the world.

☎ *(800) 346-5055 (Christian)*

## Easton

**Easton** makes its top quality Easton aluminum hockey sticks in Van Nuys, Calif.

☎ *(800) 347-3901 (Easton)*

## Reidell

**Reidell** makes every pair of its top quality hockey, figure and speed skates in Redwing, Minn. The company also makes roller boots for dry land skating.

# In-Line Skating Equipment

## Rollerblade®

**Rollerblade Inc.** pioneered the modern sport of in-line skating. Rollerblade® skates were originally created as an off-season training tool for hockey players. Later, skiers, cyclists and runners discovered the cross-training benefits of Rollerblade® skates. Today, all sorts of people in-line skate for fun and fitness on a wide variety of skates, but the original Rollerblade® brand skates are still considered the best that money can buy.

All Rollerblade® skates are manufactured in Minnetonka, Minn. Most Rollerblade **Blade Gear® Apparel** is also manufactured in the United States.

☎ *800-232-ROLL (Rollerblade)*

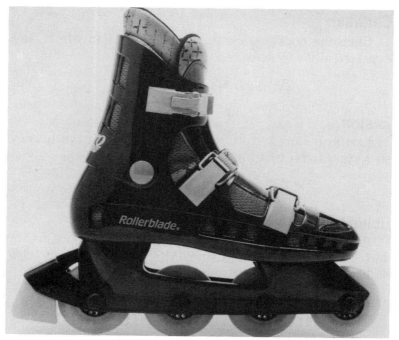

*The "Aero Blade" by Rollerblade®*

# Bowling Balls

## Brunswick

**Brunswick** is the world's largest manufacturer of bowling products. Brunswick bowling balls are made in Muskegon, Mich., as are some of the company's bowling bags. These bags are labeled "made in the U.S.A."

## Ebonite

**Ebonite,** which has had more recent patents than anyone else in the industry, manufactures its famous bowling balls in Hopkinsville, Ky.

# Boxing Equipment

## Everlast

**Everlast** is the world's most famous name in boxing equipment. The company was the official supplier of boxing equipment for the 1984 Olympic Games in Los Angeles. The list of champions who have used Everlast equipment is a veritable who's who of boxing's greatest: Jack Dempsey, Rocky Marciano, Muhammad Ali, Marvelous Marvin Hagler.

Everlast gloves retail for $38-$200 and include children's gloves and the newest in thumbless gloves— which are said to reduce eye and hand injuries and facial lacerations. The company also makes a complete selection of punching bags, uniforms, cups and headgear.

It is even possible to purchase a full size boxing ring from Everlast. Prices range from $8,800 for a plain elevated ring to $15,000 for an official Olympic ring.

All Everlast boxing equipment is made in New York and Missouri.

☎ *(800) 221-8777 (Everlast)*

# Volleyball Sets

## Centerline Sports

**Centerline** makes "the last volleyball system you'll ever need." The company offers several complete volleyball sets, including a special sand kit for beach games. All sets include durable, portable nets, stakes and poles, boundary lines and carrying bags. Centerline volleyball systems are manufactured in Denver, Colo.

☎ *(800) 451-3710 (Centerline)*

# Horseshoes

## St. Pierre

President Bush's favorite pastime is also one of the most American. The world's largest manufacturer of horseshoes, **St. Pierre Manufacturing,** is located in Worcester, Mass. The company manufactures eight different models, all of which are approved by the National Horseshoe Pitching Association. St. Pierre horseshoes are 100 percent American, including the steel in the shoes.

☎ *(508) 853-8010 (St. Pierre)*

# Outdoor and Camping Equipment

Americans love to leave their cities and home towns behind and explore the simple pleasures of the out-of-doors. Of course, people have many different ideas of the best way to "get away from it all." Some like to spend the weekend relaxing in a nearby state park. Others prefer to spend a week backpacking or canoeing in the remotest of national forests and wilderness areas. Whatever your tastes in outdoor adventure, U.S. companies can supply you with the necessary equipment and clothing.

Our research staff has recently begun to examine U.S. companies producing quality outdoor equipment stateside. In 1993, the Foundation will present an entire chapter on outdoor and camping equipment. What follows is a sneak preview focusing on the best of American-made tents and a few all-American outdoor innovations.

# Tents

The high-quality U.S. tent market is dominated by a few names: Bibler, Eureka, Jansport, Kelty, Moss, The North Face, Sierra Designs and Walrus.

The two "big names" that **do not** manufacture any of their tents in the U.S. are Jansport and Sierra Designs. The remainder of the big name manufacturers make some or all of their tents in the U.S.

## Bibler

All **Bibler** tents are hand-built in Boulder, Colo. Bibler is the only manufacturer in the U.S. making functional single wall tents. Bibler's dome-style tents are constructed from a single wall of "ToddTex"® fabric that is made exclusively for Bibler. This unique fabric makes Bibler tents extremely lightweight and waterproof yet breathable. Bibler tents range from solo models to four-person tents and are priced from $450-$850.

☎ *(303) 449-7351 (Bibler)*

## Moss

*The Moss "Olympic"*

Every **Moss** tent is manufactured by this small company in Camden, Maine. Moss tents, which run anywhere from $300 to $765, are expedition grade tents that are known for their innovation, design and patterning. Loyal Moss customers can be found in all parts of the world, including Japan, Canada, Germany, Switzerland and Belgium.

☎ *(800) 341-1557 (Moss)*

## Eureka

Eureka is a division of **Johnson Camping Co.**, which manufactures most of its products overseas. The vast majority of Eureka tents are manufactured in Korea—including Eureka's line of family tents. However, Eureka still makes a few of its best tents in the U.S.

Eureka's **Timberline-Deluxe** tents are available in both two- and four-person, regular and camouflage models. They are strong, lightweight and easily assembled, and are well-suited (although a bit heavy) for backpacking. Prices range from $190-$280. Although these tents are relatively expensive, they will outlast and outperform their imported counterparts. Note only the Timberline **Deluxe** models are made in the States.

The Eureka **Outfitter four-season Timberline tents** are rugged tents available in two-, four-, and six-person models. These tents are designed to take a beating and are ideal for groups, rentals and expeditions. An Outfitter could easily be used as a dependable U.S.-made family tent. Prices are just above those of the Timberline-Deluxe.

☎ *(800) 572-8822 (Eureka)*

## The North Face

**The North Face** is based in Berkely, Calif., and manufactures top quality, but consequently expensive, four-season tents here in the U.S. (Four-season tents are designed to withstand the rigors of year-round camping—including winter camping.) These tents range from $385-$795 and are well-made, dependable tents for the serious outdoors enthusiast.

The North Face manufactures all of its three-season tents overseas. Although the company will introduce a new line of family tents this year, these will also be manufactured abroad.

## Kelty

**Kelty** manufactures only upper-end, expedition grade four-season tents in the U.S. These are the **Jetstream, Windface II and III** and the **Microfoil**. These Kelty tents are excellent, albeit expensive ($400-$675) tents.

☎ *(800) 423-2320 (Kelty)*

## Walrus

This Berkely, Calif., company makes all of its four-season tents—the **Moonrock** ($475), **Apogee** ($650) and **Eclipse** ($750)—in the U.S. The rest of Walrus tents are made overseas.

☎ *(510) 526-8961 (Walrus)*

# American Innovations in Outdoor Equipment

## Therm-A-Rest Sleeping Pads

Sleeping outdoors can make for a "hard" night's sleep. For many, ordinary sleeping pads just don't seem to make the ground any softer.

**Cascade Designs** of Seattle Wash., solved this problem in 1973 when the company introduced its **Therm-A-Rest** foam-filled, bonded, air filled sleeping pads. These extremely comfortable, self-inflating mattresses were designed by a former Boeing aircraft engineer. They are available in a range of styles including 3/4, Ultra-lite and wider, thicker Camp Rest models and are suitable for adults, children, weekend campers and serious outdoors enthusiasts alike. Although Therm-A-Rest mattresses retail for about $50, they are priceless, required pieces of equipment for anyone sleeping in the out-of-doors.

Cascade Designs also manufactures an innovative **Ridge Rest** foam pad, which is a more affordable alternative to a Therm-A-Rest. This foam pad is a simple, light-weight and inexpensive sleeping pad ($15) that features specially molded, ridged foam. These pads are much more durable and comfortable than regular foam pads and were ranked by *Backpacker Magazine* as one of the 10 best designed outdoor products in 1988.

All Cascade Design products are manufactured in Seattle, Wash.

☎ *(800) 531-9531 (Cascade Design)*

## The Crazy Creek Chair

Crazy Creek portable "chairs" provide a dry comfortable seat no matter where you go. These lightweight (20 oz.) coated Cordura chairs can be folded and taken anywhere. They are great for picnics, backpacking, bicycle touring, camping or a trip to the stadium. They can even be converted into a sleeping pad.

*A Crazy Creek "Power Lounger"*

These revolutionary chairs were invented by two U.S. Outward Bound instructors in 1988. The chairs were an immediate hit and have become practically standard equipment for anyone who spends time outdoors—including those in Japan, Norway, Germany and a variety of other countries. The pair's company, **Crazy Creek Products**, manufactures Crazy Creek chairs in Red Lodge, Mont.

☎ *(406) 446-3446 (Crazy Creek)*

# Furniture

## The Industry

The United States produces an endless variety of furniture. From Early American to modern, U.S.-made Italian and "crate" style furniture, U.S.-made furniture comes in every style and every price range. What follows is a brief discussion of some of the best American furniture manufacturers in Early American, Georgian, U.S.-made Italian and contemporary styles of furniture. But first, a word on furniture wood.

The United States is blessed with an abundance of quality hardwood trees that form the backbone of the U.S. furniture industry. Although U.S. forests are cut for a range of high demand products, including paper, lumber and other wood products, U.S. timbers companies typically replant trees as they cut them down. This leaves the U.S. with a plentiful supply of beautiful furniture-quality wood.

Many consumers are unaware of this rich supply and cannot distinguish between imported and domestic wood furniture. To make sure that your American-made wood furniture contains domestic wood, watch for the following wood types:

### American Wood
*Pine*
*Oak (red and white)*
*Maple*
*Bird's Eye*
*Walnut*
*Spruce*

*Birch*
*Beech*
*Aspen*
*Poplar*
*Ash*
*Cedar*
*Cherry*
*Elm*
*Douglas Fir*

Purchasing American wood furniture has many benefits. It not only supports the U.S. timber industry but is usually far cheaper than exotic wood furniture. It can also be more ecological than purchasing foreign wood furniture. Much European sourced designer furniture (and a fair amount of American-made wood furniture) is crafted from wood taken from the rainforests. As is well known, the world's rain forests, crucial to the atmosphere and health of the global environment, are being depleted at a dangerous pace. Purchasing furniture made from rainforest wood contributes to the decline of the environment.

Here are some of the most popular rainforest woods:

## Rainforest Wood
*Teak*
*Mahogany*
*Ebony*
*Rosewood*
*Zebrawood*

# Early American

## Kittinger Co.

**Kittinger Co.** is a top-line manufacturer of Early American style furniture. The company began in 1885 in Buffalo, N.Y., where it attracted many skilled Polish, German and Italian immigrant craftsmen and began earning its reputation for impressive high quality furniture.

From 1969 to 1972, Kittinger refurbished the presidential offices in the West Wing of the White House. During that period, the State Department gave Kittinger furniture as gifts to visiting dignitaries. The white damask chairs that President Reagan sat in for many of his photo sessions were not produced in colonial Massachusetts, but Kittinger's Buffalo factory.

☎ *(716) 867-1000 (Kittinger)*

*The H-Bombe secretary bookcase (l) and T448 stand-up desk (r)
from Kittinger*

## Lane Furniture Manufacturers

**Lane,** one of America's largest furniture manufacturers, produces a dramatically different style of furniture than Kittinger. While much of Kittinger's Early American furniture emphasizes elaborate detail, Lane, strongly influenced by the folk art of the Shakers, stresses the plain and functional. Shakers are small religious communities from Maine to Ohio that believe in common ownership of property and a strict and simple way of life. Naturally, their furniture is simply stated and, some might say, austere.

While originally known for cedar chests and then simply styled "Shaker" furniture, Lane's contemporary offerings include more than 80 reproductions and adaptations of antique furniture approved by the Museum of American Folk Art.

*Day bed from "America" Collection by Lane*

# Georgian

Georgian furniture was produced in 18th-century England during the reigns of King George I to King George III. It is an ornate style that is sometimes similar to English-inspired Early American furniture, especially the Williamsburg variety.

## Kittinger

In addition to the Early American reproductions mentioned above, Kittinger manufactures the **Georgian Collection**.

## Drexel Heritage

Drexel Heritage is one of North Carolina's finest furniture companies. Heritage's **Heirlooms** line is a collection of Georgian reproductions.

## Baker

Another top manufacturer of Georgian reproductions is the **Baker** company of Grand Rapids, Michigan. Its collections are copied from British antiques selected by Sir Humphrey Wakefield, a noted antique authority.

## Bernhardt Furniture Co.

This company, based in Lenoir, N.C., has over 50 hand-carved Georgian designs in its **Centennial Collection**. These pieces are carved from solid mahogany and other woods and demonstrate careful attention to the detail of the English originals.

☎ *(704) 758-9811 (Bernhardt)*

*Dining table, china deck and credenza from Bernhardt's*
*"Centennial Collection"*

# Italian—
# Made in the USA

## Casa Stradivari

Old world craftsmen are alive and well in Brooklyn, N.Y. A family owned and operated business, **Casa Stradivari** has manufactured its furniture by hand for four generations. All Casa Stradivari wooden furniture is glued and carved by hand and then sanded, stained,

*A Casa Stradivari chair*

hand-burnished, lacquered, rubbed with steel wool and polished into a work of art.

☎ *(800) 233-1233 (Casa Stradivari)*

# Contemporary American Furniture

## Brayton International

*"Danube" loveseat and chair from Brayton*

This 19-year-old-company produces international design furniture in High Point, N.C. Brayton has won numerous design awards, including the Roscoe Design Award and the Stuttgart Design Center Award.

☎ *(919) 434-4151 (Brayton)*

## The Pace Collection

This company manufactures desks, tables, cabinets and other high-quality contemporary furniture. Pace manufactures many pieces in Europe as well. Pace's furniture is extremely expensive, but includes some of the best quality money can buy.

*The Pace "K" desk*

The **Mezzaluna Executive Desk** is half-moon shaped and made out of stainless steel. Designed by Leon Rosen, it sells for $20,000. The **K Desk**, designed by Steven Holl, is made out of ash, and sells for $6,000.

## Jack Lenor Larsen

Although headquartered in New York City, **Larsen** manufactures and sells its products world-wide. The company maintains showrooms in 18 countries.

*From Jack Lenor Larsen:*
*Baldwin Channeled Lounge Chair*

American designer Ben Baldwin created the Baldwin Channel chair and couch and the Cranbrook lounge chair, which is also available as a couch.

☎  *(212) 674- 3993 (Larsen)*

## R Jones and Associates
A relative newcomer to the furniture business, **R Jones & Associates** has a quality and style that make it a stand-out from its more established peers. Its factory is located in Dallas, Texas, itself a new home to quality furniture manufacturing. R Jones produces more than 100 series of couches, loveseats, chairs and beds.

☎  *(214) 951-0091 (R Jones and Associates)*

## Aristocrat Upholstery
**Aristocrat Upholstery** of Bridgeport, Pa., manufactures high quality upholstered furniture. Most Aristocrat furniture is sectional and ideal for large living rooms. From gently curving pieces to rectangles, Aristocrat is American furniture to look for.

☎  *(215) 277-4500 (Aristocrat)*

# Mid-Priced

## Thomasville and Bassett
**Thomasville** and **Bassett** are two major U.S. manufacturers of mid-priced furniture that offer good value for the dollar. Both of these companies provides a complete range of styles, from Early American to modern, from Chinese to country. A complete bedroom of Bassett furniture ranges from $1,000 to $2,000. Thomasville is somewhat higher priced.

# Leather

You don't have to buy Italian to find high quality leather furniture. American companies manufacture fine leather furniture for every pocketbook.

## Brayton

The **Brayton International Collection** includes top-end leather furniture. Brayton's **Danube** chair runs from $2,500 to $3,000 depending on the grade of leather.

## Leathercraft

**Leathercraft** produces top-quality leather furniture for less than half the price of Brayton International.

 *(704) 322-3305 (Leathercraft)*

## Craftwork Guild and Classic Leather

Both **Craftwork Guild** and **Classic Leather** are owned by Classic Leather of Hickory, N.C., and manufacture good quality leather furniture. Their furniture is slightly less expensive than Leathercraft.

*A Leathercraft sofa*

☎ *(704) 322-6365 (Craftwork Guild)*

☎ *(704) 328-2046 (Classic Leather)*

# Crate

"Crate" Furniture is a relatively new phenomenon in American furniture. Introduced to the public a decade ago, it has since achieved wide popularity. Crate furniture is made out of solid pine and is reminiscent of wooden packing crates. Its simplicity, durability and functionality is also reminiscent of Shaker style furniture. Crate furniture is ideal for families with young children who need furniture that can take abuse. Prices are generally modest.

ARTWORK

*This End Up "Crate" style bunkbeds*

The following companies are major American manufacturers of crate furniture. All of their furniture is made in the U.S.A.

**This End Up** — Raleigh, N.C. ☎ *(800) 638-2234*

**Pine Factory** — Ashland, Va. ☎ *(800) 433-7259*

**Cargo Factory** — Shase City, Va. ☎ *(800) 333-1402*

# ★☆ 12 ☆★
# Rugs and Carpets

## Nylon

Nylon is a cheap and popular form of carpeting. Ninety percent of the carpeting sold in the U.S. is made of nylon, and virtually every square yard of it is made in the States.

Most nylon carpets are constructed from Dupont's Stainmaster carpet fibers. Consequently, determining the quality of a nylon carpet is not based on fibers, as it is with wool carpets, but on density. The more a yard of carpet weighs, the more fiber it contains and the higher its quality.

There are many U.S. companies making quality nylon carpets in the U.S. The best way to shop for qulaity American-made nylon carpeting is follow the density rule of thumb.

One company to note is **Patcraft** of Dalton, Ga. This company produces a marvelous collection of nylon patterned carpets.

☎ *(404) 277-2133 (Patcraft)*

## Wool

In spite of the fact that wool carpets are more expensive than nylon, they are still popular with American consumers. The only significant carpet imports into the U.S. are oriental rugs. However, American carpet manufacturers have developed new technologies to compete with imported orientals. In 1948, Edward Fields developed the "magic needle" process, which produces "handmade" carpets by machine. More recently, Karastan developed a computerized system for making oriental-style rugs right here in the U.S.

## Karastan

Karastan produces more wool carpeting than any other manufacturer in the United States. It specializes both in broadloom and oriental-style carpeting. In fact, as was noted above, Karastan was the first manufacturer to produce oriental-style carpets in the states—by computer.

Karastan's computer organizes a pattern of various colors of yarn into a "cake" in which all the yarns—which are parallel to each other—are assembled into an organized pattern. All of Karastan's designs are produced using this patented computerized process, including its famed **Garden of Eden** flowers.

The quality of Karastan rugs is so high that the rugs come with a 20-year warranty and no rug has ever been returned because of improper wear.

Karastan prices are commendable. The "Medallion Serapi" oriental design carpet, shown below, retails for about $800—a far greater value than a similar carpet imported from Iran or Turkey.

☎ *(919) 665-4000 ( Karastan )*

## Edward Fields Designs

While Karastan is famous for its unique manufacturing process, **Edward Fields Designs** is well-known for its patterns. Fields offers more than 2,000 designs—the largest selection in the industry—and can custom make any carpet that a patron wishes. Fields' designs have a broad range, from modern to conservative and everything in between.

*A computer-generated Medallion Serapi design by Karastan*

*"Summer Breeze"—an Edward Fields custom design carpet*

The company's designers include some of the most illustrious names in the business, from industrial designer Raymond Loewy to New York artist Al Hirschfeld. Like Karastan, Fields uses machines to produce a "handmade" effect. Fields' machine, developed in the 1940s, is known as the "magic needle" and is famed worldwide for its performance. Fields' rugs grace, among other places, the White House, palaces, public buildings and countless celebrities' homes, planes and yachts.

Fields' rugs are not marketed in stores, but are available in showrooms in 11 cities nationwide. A typical Fields all-wool rug sells between $4,000 and $5,000 and retails for about $4,500 in a six-by-nine-foot size.

☎ *(212) 310-0400 (Fields)*

## U.S. Axminster

**U.S. Axminster** is the largest and most prestigious manufacturer of axminster carpets in the world. U.S. Axminster carpets, which are noted for their design and color quality, are found in many hotel lobbies and restaurants.

*A U.S. Axminster carpet*

The company offers unlimited numbers of colors, with some carpets sporting as many as 50. U.S. Axminster primarily custom manufactures patterned axminsters for commercial customers in wool and wool blends. Fourteen different axminster designs for the home are sold under the **Mohawk** name.

☎ *(800) 554-6637 (Mohawk)*

# Woven Wool

Woven rugs, like other types of carpeting, come in various qualities, but generally are more expensive and longer lasting.

### Native American Rugs

Hand-loomed woven rugs are still being produced by American Indians. Every one of these rugs is unique, and many are extremely beautiful.

### Wilton Rugs

Wilton rugs are machine-woven loop carpets with intricate patterns and known for being extremely long-lasting.

**Bloomsberg Carpet Co**. is one of the only manufacturers of Wilton rugs in the United States.

☎ *(800) 336-5582 (Bloomsberg)*

# 13

# Beer and Wine

## By Ben Giliberti

*Ben Giliberti is the beer and wine connoisseur for the **Washington Post** and is committed to furthering appreciation of American beer and wine.*

The American market for beer and wine is one of the most open in the world. The U.S. charges a relatively small duty—13 cents a case—on imported beer. Other nations charge a great deal more. For example, Holland, Germany and England charge U.S. companies $2.93 a case to export beer into their countries. China charges U.S. exporters an extraordinary duty of $14 a case. For years, our Canadian neighbor refused to allow U.S. beer to be sold in its provinces. Wine duties are similarly discriminatory against American products.

So every time you order or purchase beer or wine, think about the unfair treatment U.S. brewers receive overseas and choose American.

## Great (and Good) American Beers

One of the most exciting developments in the U.S. beer industry has been the arrival within the past 10 years of several dozen so-called "micro-breweries," most of which are wholeheartedly devoted to producing quality beers that can compete with the top offerings from Germany, Holland, England, Ireland and Belgium.

Many of these micro-breweries make their beers under contract with already existing breweries. Once the brand is established, however, many of these initially mom-and-pop operations graduate to their own facilities. Indeed, two of the finest producers, Boston Brewing Co., the producer of Sam Adams beers, and New Amsterdam Beer started as contract breweries, but have since opened up their own breweries.

Like the rest of the world's beers, American beers can be divided into two major types. Bottom fermenting beers, which include the familiar pilsener, ambers and bocks, are made from yeasts that settle to the bottom during fermentation. Top fermenting beers, which include ales, porters and stouts, are made from floating yeasts and tend to be fuller and heartier and deeper colored than bottom fermenters.

Though there are vast numbers of American beers worth trying, the following is my list of standouts, in order of quality. (The type of beer and location of brewing are indicated in parentheses.)

*Samuel Adams Boston Lager (amber, Massachusetts)*
*Sierra Nevada Pale Ale; Sierra Nevada Bigfoot (ale)*
*Anchor Steam Beer (amber, California)*
*Collin County Pure Gold (pilsener, Texas)*
*Boulder Extra Pale Ale (ale, Colorado)*
*Collin County Black Gold (boch, Texas)*
*Sierra Nevada Summerfest (amber, California)*
*Kessler Bock (bock, Montana)*
*Boulder Porter (porter, Colorado)*
*Dock Street Beer (Philadelphia)*
*New Amsterdam (amber, New York)*
*Sierra Nevada Stout (stout, California)*
*Kessler Lorelei (pilsener, Montana)*
*Cold Spring Export (pilsener, Minnesota)*
*Anchor Porter (porter, California)*
*Rhomberg Classic Pale Ale (ale, Iowa)*

Mass market American beers, most of which are heavily advertised, are well-made and consistent, though they tend toward uniformity.

Among the larger volume producers, here are the standouts:

**Augsberger** *(Wisconsin)*
*Erlanger's (owned by Strohs)*
*Stroh's Signature*
*Michelob (Anheuser-Busch)*

# American Wine

Virtually all American wines have European counterparts made from the same grape varieties with many or all of the same classic flavors. If you understand the wine regions of Europe, finding an American counterpart with similar classic varietal characteristics is a simple matter.

But bear in mind that "counterpart" does not mean "clone," and "similar" hardly means "identical." A California cabernet may be made from the same grapes as a sturdy French Medoc, but each has its own special strengths. Understanding these differences as well as the similarities can open up a whole new world of wine appreciation for all who enjoy great wine. And in many cases, the American alternative is less expensive and offers better value.

The focus of this chapter will be on the best American wines in each category, for that is where a country earns its reputation for greatness. Mention will also be made of less costly examples of these same varieties of wine, for that is where a country develops its reputation for value. To be sure, America offers a wine for every palate and every pocketbook.

# Cabernet Sauvignon

In recent years sophisticated wine drinkers have come to know "cigar box" aromas from Pauillac, leather and tobacco tastes from Grave, spicy perfume from Margaux and the distinctive *gout de terroir* ("taste of the soil") of the other great Bordeaux regions. But nowadays, with the dollar/franc equation more in their favor, California's top vintners are hoping for a rediscovery of the distinctive flavors of America's own great cabernets.

The term "Rutherford dust" was coined by the legendary winemaker Andre Tchelistcheff, the architect of the great Beaulieu George de Latour Private Reserve cabernets, to characterize the spicy, minty and eucalytpus-like flavors and aromas of the cabernet products in what may be America's most distinguished vineyard area, the Rutherford Bench. As a meaningful tasting term, "Rutherford dust" has been damned as much as praised. But at least it highlights what almost everyone seems to admit: The Bench is special.

Nowhere is the gathering of America's cabernet elite more conspicuously in evidence than on this four-mile stretch of gravelly loam in the heart of Napa. With every step along Highway 29, Napa's famous tourist wine road that separates the Bench from the rest of the valley, one seems to come upon another member of California's cabernet aristocracy. **Beaulieu George de Latour Private Reserve; Robert Mondavi Reserve; Heitz Martha's Vineyard; Freemark Abbey Bosche;** the **Inglenook Reserve Cask Cabernets;** and most recently, **Rubicon,** from the **Niebaum-Coppola vineyard.**

What's special here is the soil. The Bench soil lends an extra dimension—the sense of place and the taste of the soil—that comes through in wine from a specific *terroir* ("microclimate"). The Bench's magnificent profusion of superb cabernets from vineyards in close quarters provides an opportunity that is truly rare: the chance to explore the interplays of soil and winemaking in determining the greatness and character of wine.

Perhaps the most famous single American vineyard is Martha's Vineyard, which hugs the foothill of the Mayacamas Mountains, far back from the highway. The crusty Joe Heitz has made the wine here since 1966, and the **Heitz 1984 Martha's Vineyard** displays every bit of the famous, some might say notorious, Martha's Vineyard eucalyptus and mint bouquet. Very ripe and loaded with tannin, this is one to lay down.

Martha's gnarled old cabernet vines came initially from cuttings from two tiny experimental plots superbly positioned between Martha's Vineyard and the **Robert Mondavi Reserve** vineyards. The property of the wine school of the University of California at Davis, the two experimental vineyards also supplied the grapes for the **1985 Long Cabernet Sauvignon** ($30). Though still young and massive, it may be among the finest wines of the vintage.

The 1985 Long surely faces stiff competition from the **1985 Robert Mondavi Reserve** ($20-$25). Though slightly lighter than the Long, the Mondavi is a classic Rutherford cabernet, with warm, fleshy fruit and round tannins. More classically structured, with deep, sculptured fruit is the suave **1985 Far Niente** ($25), a first growth quality wine from an emerging superstar next door to Mondavi.

Moving north past the Robert Mondavi winery, the Bench soil remains the same, but a gentle warming trend occurs, yielding, at least in theory, slightly richer wines. At this point of the Bench a bold revival is underway. Napa pioneer Gustave Niebaum's three principal vineyards, which produce the great pre- and post-prohibition **Inglenook Reserve Cask cabernets,** are once again producing wine as fine as any in Napa.

From the former Niebaum "estate" vineyard, far back toward the foothills, filmmaker Francis Ford Coppola has directed the production of the stunning **1982 Rubicon** ($34), a massive, black, richly flavored cabernet sauvignon and cabernet franc blend with tremendous aging potential. From directly in front of the Inglenook winery, the richer, less gravelly soil of the Inglenook Ranch vineyard has supplied most of the cepage for the 1984 Inglenook Reserve Cask Cabernet ($12-$15). This supple, minty, very fruity offering has become one of California's hottest cabernets since its medal-winning performance at a recent California Wine Experience. The **1983 Inglenook Reunion Cabernet** for the first time in 20 years combined production from Niebaum-Coppola, Inglenook Ranch and Napanook, Niebaum's third major vineyard to the south near Yountville, duplicating the blend of the legendary Inglenooks of the past.

Those who question the aging ability of California cabernets need only experience the cabernets produced since 1936 on the DePins vineyard north of the present and former Inglenook properties. The **Beaulieu George Latour Private Reserve 1985** ($20) produced from DePins is a totally different wine from the Inglenook, much oakier and backward, but with a more classic structure—more like Bordeaux.

What a contrast to the quintessentially Californian **Freemark Abbey 1985 Bosche** ($24). Experts have rated the Bosche vineyard, adjacent to DePins, among the very best of Napa.

Nowhere is that more true than in the case of the Martha's Vineyard dead ringer **1986 Johnson-Turnbull Cabernet** ($17), as eucalyptus-like as anyone could want, at far less money than the Heitz offering. Particularly fine also is the **Cakebread Cellars 1986 Cabernet** ($17), produced next door to Johnson-Turnbull. No mintiness here, but instead, delicate pure fruit and a sweet bouquet that calls to mind a well-made young Margaux. Honorable mentions must also go to the delicious, spicy **1985 Sequoia Grove** ($12); the well-made, but closed in **1984 Flora Springs** ($12); and the very lush and deep Robert Pepi 1984 **"Vine Hill Ranch"** ($14). Best buy honors go to **Franciscan 1985 Estate Cabernet** ($7-$9).

# Chardonnay, The American White Burgundy

Frenchman Michel Laroche admits that he has lately become an unabashed admirer of a California chardonnay. That might not be notable were Laroche not also the owner of Domaine Laroche, one of France's leading producers of grand cru chablis. The chardonnay is from the Les Pierres vineyard and is made by what may be the Golden State's hottest winery, **Sonoma Cutrer.** Many have likened the style of Sonoma Cutrer to that of grand cru chablis and other premium white burgundies, all of which are made from the chardonnay.

Laroche approves of Sonoma Cutrer's blend of traditional and modern methods. Some techniques, like use of the cooling tunnel, merely duplicate the natural cooling effects of Chablis' northerly climate, he said. Others represent advances that he is considering instituting himself. Laroche says Sonoma Cutrer has what he looks for in a great wine— balance. Sonoma Cutrer has acidity balanced with fruit "in a more austere, French style," he said.

Laroche firmly believes that there is a market for American wines like Sonoma Cutrer in France. Laroche regularly uses Sonoma Cutrer as the mystery wine in his blind tastings. He reported that his tasters were not only confounded most of time, but were also very impressed.

Of recent vintages, the **1985 Les Pierres** ($19 retail) is extraordinary, but the recent **1986 Cutrer** ($19) and **1987 Russian River** ($13) bottlings are also of high quality. The Les Pierres should be aged for several years, and the others can also benefit from aging.

Some of the best chardonnays:

**Matanzas Creek "Sonoma County" 1985-86** ($15): Topflight, perfumed, appley bouquet. Very concentrated, exuberant fresh fruit flavors lightly seasoned with vanilla oak. Superb efforts that will improve for a year or more, but delightful now. The fine 1986 is more open and more ready now.

**La Crema Reserve 1986** (California; $17): Captivating, spicy, powerful new oak bouquet. On the palate, full fruit flavors overlayed with very toasty oak and buttery notes. French style chardonnay that is ready to drink now.

**Burgess Cellars Vintage Reserve 1986** (Napa; $10-$11): Worthy sucessor to the fine 1985. Recalls a good Mersault. Intriguing earthy, burgundian nose. Much toasty oak and complex fruit on the palate.

**Beaulieu Los Carneros Reserve 1986** (Napa; $11-$13): Fully realizing the potential of its superb Carneros vineyards, Beaulieu has given us this marvelously refined chardonnay loaded with soft fruit, and with a long finish. A charmer.

**Pine Ridge Knollside Cuvee 1986** (Napa; $13-$14) Exceedingly well-made, distinctive smoky bouquet and intriguing gingery notes on the palate. Excellent for current drinking.

**Beringer Napa Valley 1986** ($10-$12): Tasted against the finest chardonnays, this 40 percent barrel-fermented wine didn't betray its modest price in the least. Spicy, yeasty bouquet. Well-structured, savory fruit and lively acidity. Long finish. Definite short-term aging potential.

**William Hill Reserve 1986** (Napa; $13-$18): Refined, complex, understated style of chardonnay with the balance to age well. One or more years' cellaring suggested.

Other excellent chardonnays:

**Kalin Cellars Cuvee LV 1985** ($18)
**Raymond Napa Valley 1986** ($12)
**Clos Du Bois Proprietor's Reserve 1986** ($25-$30)
**Hanna 1987** ($15)
**Hacienda Clair de Lune 1987** ($12)
**Saintsbury Carneros 1986** ($12-$13)
**Monticello Corley Reserve 1987** ($13-$14)
**Mazzocco Vineyards 1986** ($12)
**De Loach Russian River 1987** ($13)
**Sanford Santa Rosa County 1985** ($15)

**Fetzer Sundial 1987** ($8-$9)
**Kendall-Jackson Proprietor's Reserve 1986** ($25)
**Callaway Calla-Lees 1987** ($9-$10)
**Prince Michel Barrel Select 1986** ($18)
**St. Francis 1986** ($9.50)
**Wente Arroyo Seco Reserve 1985** ($10)
**Concannon Selected Vineyard 1985** ($9)

## *Champagne and Sparkling Wines*

For many wine drinkers, it's French champagne—or settling for second best. Savvy wine consumers are putting this "accept no substitutes" point of view aside and trying the worthiest challengers from the U.S.

Many of the best new releases from California are priced below the level of French champagne. The line between French and American champagne is beginning to blur. In recent years, leading French champagne houses have invested heavily in the United States, setting up shop with wineries and vineyards in Napa, Carneros, Anderson Valley and elsewhere in the Golden State. The progeny, which include Domaine Mumm, Roederer Estate, Maison Deutz, Piper Sonoma and Domaine Chandon, stack up quite well against their parents.

One California-French hybrid that can surely hold its own with the world's best is **Roederer Estate.** It's a dead ringer for French champagne. Roederer Estate's fruit is from the Anderson Valley.

Compared to California sparklers, French champagnes show more pronounced yeasty, biscuity and toasty flavors. Most California sparkling wines display more fruit. the high fruit levels may be California's greatest asset. Such wines are very forward and need no additional aging to show their best.

The following champagnes are recommended:

**Roderer Estate Brut** ($14; Anderson Valley): Small bubbles, toasty, biscuity flavors, lots of finesse and a hint of bright grapiness that should have, but didn't, tip me off that this was Californian. Superb. Very highly recommended.

**Iron Horse Blanc de Blancs 1984** ($24; Sonoma County, Green Valley): Pleasing, apple-like bouquet, and beautifully expressed, generous chardonnay fruit overlaid by light, tiny bubbles. Highly recommended.

**Mumm Cuvee Napa Brut Prestige** ($14; Napa): Pinkish tinge and strawberry-red burgundy-like nose reflects heavy employment of pinot noir in the cepage. Because of its high fruit level, this was least champagne-like of all the California-French offspring, but it was still well-made and pleasant. Recommended.

**Gloria Ferrer Brut** ($10-12; Napa): Active, frothy mousse; fine, mineral scented, chardonnay nose. Solid, firm and lively on the palate. Highly recommended, a best buy.

**Maison Deutz Brut** ($15; Santa Barbara): Very active mousse; austere, taut, champagne-like structure.

**Domaine Chandon Brut (Moet)** ($12; Napa): Very French-styled, in a lean, elegant style. And don't miss the tasty Domaine Chandon Reserve ($19).

**Piper Sonoma Brut** ($14): Fine smoky bouquet. On the palate, full, pinot noir dominated flavors with a nice vanilla note.

**Scharffenberger 1984 Blanc de Blancs Brut** ($18; Mendocino): Pleasantly fruity, almost grapy, but lacks the excitement of the top offerings.

## *Pinot Noir/Red Burgundy*

French red burgundy is a great wine. The problem is, there has never been enough of it, at least at prices most of us can afford.

Despite some early failures, American pinot noir is increasingly proving itself to be as high in quality as all but a handful of top French burgundies. In California, the most consistent results have come from the more temperate

Carneros region straddling Napa and Sonoma, where the best wine are truly burgundian in character.

Oregon, however, with long summer days and a northerly climate, may prove to be the true American home for the pinot noir. Its ever-improving reputation traces back to 1979, when French experts picked a 1975 Eyrie Vineyards pinot noir over several famous French burgundies at a Paris tasting. Many Oregon offerings will remind burgundy fans of a good Volnay or Beaune. The following clearly stood out:

**Saintsbury 1986 Carneros** (California; $11-$13): Immensely fruity bouquet, clean, vibrant pinot noir fruit, with moderate tannins and classic burgundian expansion of the palate. Superb value.

**Santa Cruz Mountain Vineyards 1985** (California; $15-$18): Good winemaking is evident in this rich, chewy, pinot Should you taste a bit of Pauillac or Cote Rotie in these wines, however, you'll understand my sole reservation about winemaker Ken Burnap's efforts here.

**Oak Knoll 1986 Vintage Select** (Oregon; $14): A smoky, cherry bouquet, silky, elegant fruit and firm tannins make this an ideal pinnot for drinking and enjoying now.

**Bethel Heights Willamette 1985** (Oregon; $12): Deep purple color and lush, lively raspberry fruit, and long, mouthfilling finish.

**Robert Mondavi 1984 Reserve** (California; $16-$18): The smoky, toasty oak provides a fine counterpoint to the pure pinot fruit of this offering.

**Hacienda 1985** (California; $12-$14) Nicely defined structure, and well-balanced, complex fruit.

**Soleterra 1985** (California; $14): Ripe, earthy, firmly structured and tannic style. Not particularly burgundian, but a good wine at the price.

# Light Fruity Style Wines—
# Red Zinfandel

In search of red wines for summer drinking, American wine consumers have traditionally looked to Europe rather than to our own vineyards for light, fruity and refreshing reds that can be served chilled on a hot summer day.

All but overlooked in the search have been the reds produced form that quintessentially American grape, the zinfandel. That's a shame, because when it is made in a lighter style, zinfandel can be a superb summer red, delivering generous dollops of fresh raspberry-like fruit, along with enough structure to stand up to tangy summer salads and charcoal-grilled foods. In addition, at prices as low as $4 to $5 a bottle, zinfandel represents outstanding value.

To those unfamiliar with its many incarnations, however, zinfandel may at first seem an unlikely choice for a summer red. One rather fundamental reason is that many wine consumers may be surprised to discover than red zinfandel exists at all. A whole generation of wine drinkers is more familiar with white zinfandel, which is made by fermenting ordinary red zinfandel grapes off their deeply pigmented skins to minimize color extraction. White zinfandel, which is really a rosé or blush wine, has achieved enormous commericial success, but to date little of its success has rubbed off on its red cousin, which remains a relatively slow seller compared to cabernet and merlot.

Those who try a lighter red zinfandel will find that it neatly bridges the gap between the more familiar types of zinfandel. It maintains most all of the spicy, refreshing notes that have made white zinfandel such a hit, but unlike most white zinfandels, it is fully dry and usually more complex. It also captures much of the explosive fruit of the bigger zinfandels, but its low alcohol, lighter color and less aggressive character make it a far better choice for summer drinking.

In an era when the top Beaujolais are fetching $12 or more per bottle, zinfandel captures the original spirit of Beaujolais even better than many true French Beaujolais.

By contrast, the summer zinfandels seek only to deliver lots of fresh, grapy leisure at a modest price. In this regard, they succeed splendidly. The following are my choices, listed in order of preference:

**Ravenswood 1987 Vintners Blend** ($7): Superb; bursts with wealth of raspberry fruit; harmonious balance between fruit and moderate tannins; intense without ever seeming heavy.

**Parducci Mendocino County 1986** ($6): Brilliant ruby color. Vibrant, light picnic-style zinfandel, with fresh strawberry notes on bouquet and palate, and a crisp, clean finish.

**Guenoc Lake County 1985** ($7): Spicy, elegant, claret style zinfandel with fruit that is both lush and well-focused.

**Sebastini Sonoma County 1986** ($5-$6): A real bargain; soft, grapy fruit light quaffing style perfect for patio sipping.

**Beringer North Coast 1986** ($8): Medium-weight claret style with fine complexity; impressive depth of flavor.

**Karly Amador County 1987** ($8): Outstanding depth and exuberant expression of fruit. Drink now for grapy fruit, but hold some for mellower pleasures this fall.

**Kendall-Jackson Mendocino 1986** ($7): Though not necessarily the best of Kendall-Jackson's stable of excellent zinfandels, clearly the freshest and grapiest, with some earthiness on the nose.

**Pedroncelli Sonoma County 1986** ($7): As always, good value is offered by Pedroncelli in this light- to medium-weight offering featuring ripe round fruit and a smooth finish.

**Seghesio 1985 Northern Sonoma 1985** ($6): A pleasing, lighter style; crisp and mature.

**Fetzer California 1986** ($6): Light- to medium- weight, clean strawberry flavors nicely set off by American oak notes.

**Marietta Old Vines Red Lot 7** (non-vintage; $5-$6): More muscular and dense than the fabulously successful Lot 6 offered last year. Still offers a good value, although the addition of petite sirah detracts from the former sprightliness of the wine.

## Rosés and White Zinfandels

As the accompaniment to a light summer meal served after a hot day, few wines can match the refreshing appeal of a lightly chilled rosé. Their pink to salmon color suggests how perfectly they fill the gap between reds, most of which are too heavy in summer, and whites, which lack the body to match many dishes.

Vintages hardly matter with rosés. Drink them as young as possible. They rarely improve with age. The 1986s and 1987s are at the peak. Most '85s are also fine.

The top American rosés offer a surprisingly high level of quality, complexity and value. Many can compete head to head in flavor with the best French rosés, and prices are modest, often well under $10. The best rosés:

**Bonny Doon's Vin Gris de Cigare,** produced in California by the colorful Randall Graham, is one such wine. Made from the traditional Rhone grape varieties in a bone dry format, the inspiration for this wine is the dry rosés made near the French village of Chateauneuf du Pape.

Bonny Doon's label may be the most distinctive ever stuck on a wine bottle. It's a reverse affair that can only be seen by looking through the wine. It depicts a peaceful vineyard scene—with a flying saucer hovering overhead. The inspiration for the flying saucers (*Cigare volant*) is a Chateauneuf du Pape village ordinance banning such conveyances from the skies above its vineyards.

**Bonny Doon 1988 Gris de Cigare** ($9): Made primarily from the mourvedre, the major grape of Bandol, this one is too good and too much fun to pass up. The fruit is light and expansive on the palate, with light peach and orange notes; it has the length to prove that rosés really can have a finish. The first great American rosé, and arguably the tastiest rosé made.

**Heitz Girgnolino Rose 1986** ($6): This may be the Martha's Vineyard of rosé; lots of spicy, gewurtztraminer-like character on the nose and on the palate.

**Amador Foothills 1988 White Zinfandel** ($7): Bone dry, yet loaded with fresh, strawberry-like fruit. A real gem.

**Beringer 1988 White Zinfandel** ($8): A huge seller, and it's not hard to see why. Spicy fruit, with loads of charm.

# The Challenge of American Winemaking

Having discussed American wines by grape variety, it is also important to understand what goes into American wines besides grapes. For although American wines are made from European varietals, there is a boldness to them that is distinctly American. While surely this has much to do with climate and winemaking techniques, in my view this character has less to do with these factors than with something else, more abstract, perhaps, but no less critical—the simple determination to succeed, combined with that most American of virtues—ingenuity. By all the criteria that the experts have established as necessities for great wine—for example, proper soil types, climate and grape varieties—high quality American wine should be an impossibility.

That America is not a natural breeding ground for the production of great wine might come as a shock to many of us. In some quarters, we have been led to believe that America is a winemaker's Nirvana. We are told that in California, every year is a vintage year; that the French send their winemakers here to study in our schools; that American wines constantly win in blind tastings against their European competitor.

Let's start with climate. Compared with the relatively moderate climates of Bordeaux, Burgundy, northern Italy and even Spain, the American climate looks like an obstacle course. It's too hot. The growing season is too short. The day/night temperature variation is too great. It's either too damp, as in Maryland, Virginia and Oregon, or it's a virtual desat, as in Napa and Sonoma.

To be sure, some of these conditions are great for producing tanker loads of jug wines for mass consumption, as Franzia and Gallo have shown in California's Central Valley. However, such climatic extremes are anathema to great wine.

To beat the heat, the California's vignerons have been particularly resourceful. In Napa, an American Airlines pilot turned winemaker, Tom Burgess, was among the first to move up the valley's eastern slopes in search of cooler temperatures that would allow for the slower ripening so essential to the complex chemistry of great wines. Today, almost two decades later, several of Burgess' early hillside vintages are still aging gracefully in the bottle. More recently, in the Stag's Leap area, the high quality of **Shafer Hillside Select, William Hill Reserve, Pine Ridge** and other hillside cabernets and chardonnays have further proved the wisdom of higher elevation plantings.

Those who have chosen to stay on the valley floor have not been left behind, however. Among the innovators here is the **Robert Mondavi** winery, which along with the Baron Philippe de Rothschild has introduced **Opus One.** Though sometimes categorized as a luxury item, Opus One is in fact a bold, pioneering effort in the use of canopy management— allowing the grape leaves themselves to provide shade for the hanging bunches—to control the scorching, direct California sunlight. While the jury is not yet in on the aging ability of Opus One, the recently released 1985 appears to have all the components to challenge the Bordeaux first growths in all respects save price—where the Opus is in fact less costly.

Perhaps the first to realize the limitations of our own varietals was Thomas Jefferson, who believed that palatable wines were an essential ingredient of a popular democracy. On his return from a stint in France as the American minister of trade, Jefferson swapped native American trees and pants —then very much the rage in European popular gardens— for cuttings of vines from Europe's finest vineyards, including Le Montrachet, Chateau Margaux and those of the Italian Piedmont.

Although Jefferson's own viticultural experiments in Virginia failed, there's no question who ultimately got the better of the deal. Two centuries later, American cabernet sauvignons decisively outpointed the top French bordeaux in a challenge tasting put on by the French winemakers, known as the "Judgment of Paris" tasting. By contrast, the American plants sent to Europe carried in their roots the dreaded phylloxera louse, which devastated the European vineyards. All European varieties must be grafted on to phylloxera-resistant American rootstock.

Innovation continues in East Coast vineyards as well. Little more than a decade ago, commercial winemaking barely existed in Virginia, Maryland and Pennsylvania, where they are still battling the same problems that appear to have undone Jefferson's early efforts—humidity-induced rot in the summer, and sudden vine-splitting cold snaps in the early spring.

To battle the winter chills, many local wineries have turned to winter-hearty hybrids with great success. Excellent hybrid bottlings included the crisp seyval blanc produced by Virginia's **Oakencroft Winery,** a toastier, woodier version of the same grape offered by Maryland's **Montbray Vineyards,** and the seyval blanc, vidal blanc blend put out by Pennsylvania's **Chaddsford Winery,** called **Chaddsford White,** a legitimate bargain at around $6. With regard to vinifera plantings, more careful site selection has helped to improve the odds against freezing. Examples of highly successful vinifera bottlings included recent vintages of the impressive **Prince Michel Vineyards Barrel Fermented** chardonnay and **Montdomaine Cellar's** cabernet and merlot blends.

But ingenuity and pluck are one thing. Taste is quite another. Have all these qualities given our wines a distinctively American flavor?

To my palate, they have. If there is one single characteristic that sets American wine apart from the wines of

Europe, it is their boldness. American chardonnays burst with a clean fruit that would almost be embarrassing in a white burgundy. Our cabernets won the Judgment of Paris tasting by making their French counterparts looks like black and white renditions. I can't help but feel this boldness reflects the bold ingenuity of our winemakers—and I sure like the taste of it in our wines.

## Value in American Wines

What also must be appreciated is the value offered by American wines. Are American wines underpriced? At least one well-known winemaker, Diamond Creek winery owner Al Brounstein, says the answer is yes. He priced **1987 Diamond Creek Lake Vineyard Cabernet** to carry a $100 retail price, the highest ever attached to a newly minted American wine.

Maintaining that other top wineries have underpriced their offerings compared with other world class competitors, such as Chateau Petrus and the Domaine de la Romanee Conti, Brounstein predicts that other American vintners will soon follow his lead. Other worthy $100-a-bottle candidates include Dunn Howell Mountain, Stag's Leap Cas 23 and Grace Family Vineyards, all of which sell for between $25 and $40 a bottle, as well as others, he said.

The good news for consumers is that even if Brounstein is correct, the wines he refers to represent but a tiny portion of California's premium white wine production. The Lake bottling is itself a prime example. It comes from a tiny 3/4 acre vineyard near the winery. Though as many as 200 cases are produced in abundant years, only 75 cases were produced in 1987. Because of its cool micro-climate, the vineyard's production is sold separately only in exceptionally hot years, which produce the best wine there. The most recent Lake bottling was 1984, and the only previous vintage was 1978. It has already been decided that there will be no 1988 Lake bottling.

The message is clear, however. Since prices can head only one way—up—this is a propitious moment to stock the cellar with high quality American wines. They deserve a place in any cellar that is devoted to quality wine.

# ★☆ 14 ☆★

# Food

## The Industry

The United States is one of the richest agricultural nations in the world. American food products are abundant and diverse. Because the U.S. is such a large nation, its territory covers a variety of climates and terrains. Consequently, different regions and states are known for particular food products. While many nations are limited by climate to a few food products—for example, over 50% of Japan's farmland is devoted to rice—the U.S. seems to have it all. From Maine to California and Alaska to Hawaii, the United States produces a vast assortment of excellent food.

Of all the products consumers buy, it is perhaps easiest to buy American-produced food. Most nations keep the vast majority of their food production and processing at home, and the U.S. is no exception. Shipping costs, spoilage and other factors make offshore production uneconomical. Consequently, U.S.-produced food is almost always cheaper than its imported counterparts. This is especially true of imported processed foods, which are often of the gourmet, specialty variety and are quite expensive.

Food products that come from our closest neighbors are perhaps the only exception to this American-is-cheaper rule. For example, Mexican fruits and vegetables are sold in the U.S. at very competitive prices.

In sum, when you purchase American food products you get high quality, almost unlimited diversity and bargain prices. Although it would be nearly impossible to catalogue all of the excellent foods the U.S. has to offer, here are a few suggestions to get you started eating "American".

# Bottled Water

Imported bottled water seems to be everywhere. For many, it seems to be part of an image to be seen sipping a European bottled water such as Perrier or Evian. However, it is completely unnecessary to look all the way to the south of France (Perrier) or to the Alps (Evian) to find an excellent mineral water.

The U.S. has many springs whose waters rival those from any part of the globe. Three of the best American mineral waters to choose from are **Quibell** from the Appalachians in West Virginia, **Saratoga** from the renowned Saratoga Springs in New York and **Poland Springs** from the Maine woods.

# Coffee

Believe it or not, some of the world's best coffee is made from coffee beans grown on two American islands—Hawaii and the U.S. Commonwealth of Puerto Rico. **Kona Coffee** is grown on the lush volcanic slopes of Hawaii's Kona coast. This excellent coffee is available in different grades, depending on the plantation it was grown on and the quality of the beans. Kona coffees can be found in coffee stores nationwide for $17-$20 a pound. You can also order directly from **Mauna Loa.**

☎ *(800) 832-9993 (Mauna Loa)*

Puerto Rican coffee is wonderful. It is also less expensive than Hawaiian coffees. However, because much of Puerto

Rico's coffee is kept in the commonwealth, it is often difficult to find in the states. Some specialty coffee shops carry bulk Puerto Rican coffee for approximately $8 a pound. However, be careful: "Puerto Rican" coffee often means that the beans were roasted in Puerto Rican style—but are not really from Puerto Rico. If you can find them, two prepackaged Puerto Rican coffees to look for are **Cafe Jaucano** and **Cafe Rico.**

# Produce

American produce has many advantages. It is fresh, inexpensive and easier to find than exotic imported produce. It also contains less dangerous pesticides than fruits and vegetables from many other countries. For example, although the dangerous pesticide DDT was banned in the U.S.A., it is still used in many other countries. Unfortunately, DDT often finds its way into the U.S. on imported tomatoes and other produce.

## Some of the Best American Vegetables
*New Jersey Beefsteak Tomatoes*
*Idaho Potatoes*
*Silver Queen Corn (various states)*
*California Artichokes*
*California Avocados*

## Some of the Best American Fruits and Nuts
*Florida Oranges*
*Florida Grapefruit*
*Hawaiian Pineapple*
*Macadamia Nuts (Hawaii)*
*Washington State Apples*
*New York State Apples*
*Georgia Peaches*
*Nubiana and Santa Rosa Plums (California)*
*Cranberries (Massachusetts)*
*Blueberries (Maine)*
*Cherries (Michigan)*

*Pears (Oregon)*
*Pecans (Georgia)*
*Almonds (California)*
*Pistachios (California)*
*Peanuts (Georgia and Alabama)*

All of these products can be found in your local grocery store or specially ordered through growers, their distributors or specialty companies. Here are some suggestions for direct ordering:

## California Cachet
(San Francisco, Calif.)—California fruits, nuts and wines; worldwide shipping.

☎ *(800) 422-2438*

## Indian River Citrus Specialties
Will ship Florida grapefruits directly from the grove to anywhere in the world.

☎ *(800) 223-7740*

## Melatchie Farms
(Perry, Ga.)—Georgia peaches.

☎ *(800) 241-7013*

## Maine Wild Blueberry Co.
(Machias, Maine)—Maine blueberries.

☎ *(800) 243-4005*

## Orchard Pecan
(Albany, Ga.)—Georgia pecans.

☎ *(800) 841-4350*

## Pinnacle Orchards
(Medford, Ore.)—Oregon pears.

☎ *(800) 547-0227*

# Seafood

*Alaska King Crab*
*Maine Lobster*
*Florida Stone Crabs*
*Chesapeake Bay Crabs*
*Gulf of Mexico Shrimp*
*Chincoteague Oysters*
*Pacific Salmon*
*Tuna*
*Dungeness Crabs (Pacific Northwest)*

American seafood can be found in seafood and specialty food stores across the U.S. American seafood can be directly ordered and express couriered (usually Federal Express) to almost anywhere in the world. To order some of America's best seafood, try the following companies:

## Bay State Lobster Co.
Maine lobsters; will ship live lobsters anywhere.

☎ *(800) 225-6240 or (617) 523-7960*

## Clambakes to Go
Complete New England clam bakes (an assortment of lobster, codfish, mussels, steamers, sausage, potatoes, corn and onions ).

☎ *(800) 423-4038*

## Great Maine Lobster Co.
Lobsters and lobster cooking tools.

☎ *(800) 222-5033*

## Hegg & Hegg
(Port Angeles, Wash.)—Alder smoked western salmon.

☎ *(800) 435-3474*

## Key Largo Fisheries
Florida stone crabs. Available approximately Oct. 15 to May 15 only.

☎ *(305) 451-3782*

## Nelson Crab Co.
(Tokeland, Wash.)—Dungeness crabs.

☎ *(800) 262- 0069*

## *A note on Tuna....*
Fresh tuna tastes quite different from canned tuna. However, you can't always get fresh tuna. U.S. tuna canneries are some of the cleanest in the world and produce such fine canned tunas as **Bumblebee** solid white tuna, **Chicken-of-the-Sea** and **Starkist**.

# Meats

*Beef*

American beef is the finest in the world.  The best American beef comes from the heartland of the country—the area that stretches from Illinois and Nebraska to Texas.

# Omaha Steaks International
Ships high-quality beef to your door.

☎ *(800) 228-9055 or (402) 391-3660*

# Golden Trim
Golden Trim beef, produced by Sun Land Beef Co. of Phoenix, Ariz., is lower in calories, fat and cholesterol than ordinary beef. In fact, it contains less than half the calories of the run-of-the-mill beef and is comparable to skinless chicken. The Golden Trim product line consists of 27 cuts of beef—from filet mignon to stewing meat. Golden Trim was the first fresh beef to carry the USDA "Lite" designation.

☎ *(602) 279-7977 (Golden Trim)*

### Ham
Virginia ham is an American specialty. To order a quality Virginia ham, call **Virginia Provisions Smokehouse** *(800) 443-7086,* or **Padows** (Richmond, Va.) *(800) 344-4257.*

### Turkey
Benjamin Franklin wanted to have the turkey declared the official American bird. The eagle prevailed, but turkey is the official meal of the first truly American holiday, Thanksgiving. Smoked turkey is available from **Padows** of Richmond, Va.

☎ *(800) 344-4257 (Padows)*

### Ribs
Believe it or not, no matter where you live, you can order ribs from many of the U.S.'s more famous "rib joints" simply by picking up the phone. To have a taste of the best of Memphis' famous barbecue, for example, call **Corky's** at *(800) 284-RIBS,* **The Rendezvous** at *(901) 523-2746,* or **John Will's** at *(901) 274-8000.* With a little help from Federal

Express, your ribs will arrive on your doorstep within a day
or two.

# Gift Baskets

One excellent way to support America's food specialties
is to purchase gift baskets that feature a state's or region's
best food products. Many of the items discussed above are
available in gift assortments. There are also hundreds of
companies that specialize in sending off the best of their
area's food products as gifts baskets.

For a taste of Vermont, for example, **Cold Hollow Cider
Mill** of Waterbury, Vt. ships a large assortment of gift collections featuring Vermont maple syrup, apples, cider, cheeses,
preserves and maple candy.

☎ *(800) 3-APPLES (Cold Hollow)*

Wherever you live, you can find a local farm market or
specialty food store that will package up the best of your area
and ship it off to friends who are out-of-state or in another
country. Whether your gift features products from your own
area or a distant U.S. region, your gift will help promote the
best foods that America has to offer.

# ★☆ 15 ☆★
# Gifts

This chapter is a collection of gift items that do not fit neatly into any of the other chapters. However, any of the items discussed in this book make excellent gifts.

## Pens

A pen can be the perfect gift for Mom, Dad or a recent grad. Two of the most famous names in pens are still made in the USA:

### Cross

**A.T. Cross Co.** has been making writing instruments in the United States since 1846. Today, A.T. Cross continues to manufacture all of its pens in Lincoln, R.I., and maintains a reputation as one of the world's premier writing instrument manufacturers.

The quality that goes into manufacturing Cross writing instruments is such that fewer than 2 percent are returned for replacement or repairs and all Cross writing instruments are mechanically guaranteed for life. Cross excellence is recognized the world over—these writing instruments are exported to 150 different countries.

The company sells 83 different styles of pens ranging from $13 for a chrome mechanical pencil to $800 for a 14K gold fountain pen. Cross sells four basic types of writing instruments: pencil, ballpoint, selectip and fountain pen. Each of these is sold in various styles that include chrome, gray epoxy, black epoxy, 10K gold-filled, 14K gold-filled and sterling silver. It also offers a special series for women. The Cross for women series is available in each of the mentioned styles with additional engraving and a separate soft case for each pen.

The company also markets a number of gift sets featuring either one or two writing instruments in an attractive desk top holder. The bases come in a variety of materials such as walnut, onyx and ebony. Depending on the style, these gift packages retail for between $95 and $1,280; however, the vast majority of the Cross gift sets sell for under $200, making them an affordable, interesting gift idea.

*Cross pens*

## Parker

**Parker Pen Co.**, founded in 1888 by George Parker, is another famous name in pens. Over a century later, Parker is the world leader in sales of gift and luxury pens and proudly notes that its pens have been used for many famous events, from writing the Sherlock Holmes stories to the signing of many international treaties. Parker's product line encompasses up to 150 different styles, including an extensive selection of gold, silver and lacquer luxury pens retailing for up to $3,500, more moderately priced writing instruments for under $100, and fountain pens.

Parker has plants in England, France and Janesville, Wis. The American-made Parker pens manufactured in Janesville are the **Duofold** line, which was recently brought to the U.S. from Parker's English plant (Duofolds distributed in Europe are still made in England.), the **Classic** line and the brand-new **Insignia** gift lines. Most of these pens retail for $10 to $100 and make the perfect, distinguished gift. They also carry an unconditional, worldwide guarantee. For less expensive gift needs, Parker's U.S. plant also manufactures the **Vector** ($7- $8.50) and the **Jotter** ($5-$7.50).

This year, Parker introduced a special edition pen called **The World Memorial Pen**. These pens, available in U.S.-made Duofold Black and Insignia Black, feature an emblem crafted from the smelted remains of retired U.S. and Soviet nuclear missiles. The proceeds of the sale of this pen go to support the England-based World Memorial Fund, which provides international disaster relief.

# Silver, Crystal and China

## Kirk Stieff

In 1979 two of the finest names in American silver merged to create **Kirk Stieff**, perhaps the most prestigious name in silver. Samuel Kirk first made silverware in the Baltimore area beginning in 1815. In 1820, Kirk introduced the Repousse style, which featured the distinctive flower and foliage design that has since become world famous. Early Kirk silver graced some of the finest American homes, including those of the Marquis de Lafayette, Robert E. Lee, the Astors and the Roosevelts.

Charles Stieff did not establish his firm until 1892, but was just as influential, particulary in its passage of the Silver Laws Registration. This legislation ensured that only pieces with at least 92.5 percent fine silver could legally be labeled as sterling silver. In 1939, Steiff also began crafting authentic reproductions for Colonial Williamsburg.

Thus the merger of the two companies joined two of the oldest and most respected American silver firms. Now, Kirk Stieff is among the most sought-after silver in the world.

The company crafts many different silver products, from official reproductions for the Smithsonian, Monticello, Old Sturbridge Village, Historic Charleston and Colonial Williamsburg to flatware sets. A stunning example of the best Kirk Stieff has to offer is its sterling silver Repousse waiter. This exceptionally made 22-inch tray retails for approximately $15,000.

Rest assured, only a small percentage of the Kirk Stieff catalogue falls into this price range. Kirk Stieff manufactures and sells many exquisite items that are quite reasonably priced. An excellent, inexpensive gift from Kirk Stieff might be one of its sterling silver bookmarks, which retail for $10-$20. The bookmarks are available in a boxed and a ribbon style. Another economically priced gift item is the company's letter openers ($30), which come in a variety of designs. For those interested in spending slightly more money, Kirk Stieff sells a number of picture frames in silver. The company sells both 3x5 inch ($150) and 8x10 inch ($295) frames.

Kirk Stieff silver products are crafted in Baltimore, Md, and are backed by this unconditional warranty: "Simply rest assured that if the manufacture of any Kirk Stieff product should be flawed, we are going to replace it."

☎ *(410) 338-6080 (Kirk Stieff)*

## Lenox

**Lenox** crystal and china is world renowned. Lenox makes crystal vases, glassware, dishes, candlesticks and many other beautiful pieces. Lenox also makes the highest quality china dishes, tea sets and vases. This U.S. company still manufactures all of its products in Pennsylvania, North Carolina and New Jersey.

☎ *(800) 533-8814 (Lenox)*

*A sample of Lenox china and crystal stemware*

## Steuben

**Steuben** is the another well-known name in American crystal. Although the company was founded in 1903, the modern Steuben emerged in 1933 when Arthur Houghton Jr. (a member of Corning's founding family) took over the Steuben Division. He hired John Gates and Sydney, already well known as an architect and a sculptor respectively, to develop a series of designs for the company. These designs were highly received when they were unveiled in 1935. Today the company continues to produce nine of these designs, an enduring testament to their quality. Modern-day Steuben is a subsidiary of Corning, which still produces all of its crystal in Corning, N.Y., in Steuben County.

The Steuben catalogue features hundreds of different pieces in four major categories. The first category is functional forms, which includes flower vases, dishes and bowls. Almost all the pieces in this category range in price from $250 to $700.

Steuben's line of ornaments includes a variety of offerings, including a crystal apple representing New York, a crystal and silver rendition of King Arthur's sword Excalibur and crystal pendants.

A third group in the Steuben line consists of crystal animal figurines. These pieces retail for as little as $135 or as much as $3,150.

Finally, its "major works" line features exquisite pieces employing Steuben's finest craftsmanship. Two examples of this are a piece designed to evoke a cathedral ($13,000) and a work celebrating the New York skyline ($28,500).

Steuben crystal may be mail-ordered or purchased in the company's Fifth Avenue store in New York City.

☎ *(800) 424-4240 (Steuben)*

# Watches

The Foundation has uncovered only one company still producing watches in the United States—**Hamilton Watch Co.**, which is owned by the Swiss **SMH Inc.** Hamilton produces both contemporary and classic style watches that have Swiss movements but American cases, bands and assembly. The company recently switched the hand assembly of its watches from Lancaster, Pa., to the U.S. Virgin Islands.

Hamilton's largest line of watches is its **Traditional Classics,** which are reproductions of famous watches from the 1920s through the 1950s. One of the most striking designs from this collection is the *Ventura.* Introduced as part of the world's first electric watch line, this uniquely shaped design was hailed as a work of art. Hamilton also offers an authentic reproduction of the watch produced for the 1928 World Series Champion New York Yankees, which has been faithfully reproduced to include the engraved caseback that commemorated the Yanks' victory. The *Wilshire, Benton* and *Carlisle* are some of Hamilton's classic rectangular shaped watches. The *Broadway Limited* is the one pocket watch in the Hamilton line. This watch has an authentic railroad dial that marks each minute separately in red and black numerals and comes with either an embossed image of a steam locomotive back or one that shows the mechanical movements.

**Contemporary Classics** are Hamilton's contemporary style watches. The majority of these watches are extremely accurate "chronograph" timepieces. The chronographs come with a variety of different dials, bezels and bands and are available in an impressive array of features for an analog watch. The *Wordtimer* Contemporary Classic gives the time in 24 different time zones at a single glance. By combining function and style, this watch is perfect for the business traveler.

# Sunglasses

## Ray-Ban

**Ray-Ban**, which manufactures all of its sunglasses sold in the states in the U.S., has been one of the top names in sunglasses for over 50 years.

It all started in the late twenties when the Army asked **Bausch & Lomb** of Rochester, N.Y., to develop sunglasses for its pilots. Apparently, the pilots often encountered brutal glare that caused severe headaches and nausea. Bausch & Lomb developed a green glass that cut glare, checked ultraviolet and infrared rays, and absorbed various colors of the spectrum in a way that allowed the pilots eyes to function naturally. The Army's expectations were not only filled, but greatly exceeded. In 1936, Bausch & Lomb began commercially marketing these flying glasses under the name Ray-Ban. Despite the skeptics who claimed that no one would pay $3.75 for a product that normally cost 25 cents to 50 cents, the glasses were a hit. In their first two decades, the glasses were mainly targeted at sports enthusiasts, but beginning around the time the **Wayfarer** was introduced in 1952, the sunglasses also became a fashion item, earning the prestigious Council of American Fashion Designers Award.

Sales of Ray-Bans have been aided by media exposure and by their identification with certain pop icons. For example, Wayfarer sales multiplied more than 50 times after the lead characters in the "Blues Brothers" and "Risky Business" films appeared in these sunglasses.

Bausch & Lomb's Ray-Ban sunglasses come in a variety of styles and include catalogue driving glasses, precious metal frames, leather frames, children's glasses and of course the Wayfarers. Ray-Ban's **Wings** sunglasses feature state-of-the-art lenses and a patented design that provides an ultimate level of protection.

All Ray-Ban sunglasses have glass lenses that exceed the impact resistance requirement of the Food and Drug Administration. In fact, the company tests every single one of its lenses—not just the sample test batch required by the FDA.

# Cameras

American-made cameras are a dying breed. If you are interested in purchasing an American-made camera, your choices are limited to the instant and disposable cameras discussed below. There are no longer any U.S. manufacturers of 35mm or pocket cameras.

## Kodak

**Eastman Kodak Co.** of Rochester, N.Y., has grown into a global company that manufactures all over the world. Unfortunately, Kodak no longer produces any of its cameras in the U.S. The closest thing to an American-made Kodak camera is the Star 235, which is assembled from mainly U.S. parts in Mexico. However, all **Kodak film** and its **Fling** disposable 35mm cameras are made in Rochester.

The basic Fling takes clear, focused pictures from as close as four feet at a shutter speed of 1/110 of a second. Other Fling cameras have specialized uses. The **Fling Weekend 35** is aimed at the sports-oriented user and has the power to take pictures at depths up to 12 feet. The **Fling Stretch 35** is a single use camera that takes panoramic pictures that measure

3 1/2 x 10". Fling disposable cameras sell for approximately $8-$10 (excluding the cost of developing) and must be returned in their entirety for developing.

## Polaroid

**Polariod** has been producing instant cameras in the United States for nearly half a century. Today, the company still produces the majority of its instant cameras, including the flagship **Spectra**, in eastern Massachusetts.

The Spectra combines the quality of 35mm pictures with the convenience of instant photography. This camera features sonar autofocus and a built in-flash that recharges in as little as 1/5 of a second. The viewfinder also guides the user by signalling "too close," "too far away" or "caution." The Spectra system includes a host of separately purchased accessories. There are five different auxiliary lenses to create multi-images, starbursts or other special effects. Other accessories include a radio-controlled remote allowing operation from 40 feet away and a tripod.

Polaroid also manufactures the American-made **Impulse** cameras, which are a more affordable alternative to the Spectra system. The **Impulse AF** (for autofocus) features two different autofocus systems and a direct viewfinder that shows the user exactly what will appear in the picture.

*The Polaroid "Spectra"*

In addition, all Impulse AF functions are controlled by a wafer-thin battery contained in the film pack. Polaroid also manufactures a more economical fixed-focus Impulse camera that selects the exposure via infrared light. The flash on this camera has an indoor range of four to 10 feet.

Like Kodak's, all **Polaroid** film is made in the U.S.

### A note on *Keystone cameras...*

**Keystone cameras**, which have been noted in this publication in recent years, are no longer made in the U.S.A.

# Leather Goods

American-made leather products make excellent gift items. Any person with a hectic schedule would surely appreciate a quality leather date or address book. Other good leather gift items are luggage, wallets and purses. Although many people believe most leather goods are imported, there are a number of American companies producing top quality leather goods.

### Berman Leathercraft

**Berman Leathercraft** manufactures a range of excellent leather date and address books.

### Coach

**Coach**, which is based in New York City, is one of the most well-known and respected names in the leather business. Originally only a manufacturer of small leather products, the company has been producing purses, bags and portfolios for a quarter century. Coach developed its own tanning and dying processes, which greatly enhance the leather's characteristics. Coach uses only solid brass fittings manufactured by a century-old equine products company. These factors all contribute to the high quality and classic look of Coach products.

## Hartman

**Hartman** is an American manufacturer of fine leather briefcases and luggage. Hartman's leather briefcases have received top marks from *Consumer Reports*. Hartman also makes top-quality vinyl briefcases.

## Sun Graphix

**Sun Graphix** offers a number of fine leather products to help busy people keep track of their time. These range from a full-size desktop planner ($45 in genuine leather) to a compact planner that easily fits into a shirt pocket. The larger planners also include such helpful extras as area code/time zone maps, interest rate charts, population statistics and weather charts.

## Schlessinger Brothers

A well-made leather briefcase is the type of gift that the recipient will cherish for a lifetime. Philadelphia-based **Schlessinger Brothers** has been making briefcases for almost three-quarters of a century. Schlessinger claims that its standards are so exacting that only 5 percent of the world's leather is good enough to be used in its products.

Schlessinger offers a large assortment of styles available in four different types of quality leather, including a limited number of crocodile skin cases. All Schlessinger briefcases feature a patented Schlessinger Casesetter steel spring frame, which ensures a strong, extremely durable case.

# Electric Razors

## Remington Products

**Remington** is an American success story. Before the present owner (Victor Kiam) acquired the company, Remington had lost an average of $10 million a year for the preceding three years. Kiam trimmed corporate fat, brought Remington's manufacturing operations home and cut the price of razors by a third. As a result, sales tripled and the defect rate dropped to near zero. Remington electric razors are now the second-largest selling razors in the U.S.

Remington manufactures excellent electric razors for both men and women—90% of which are made in the U.S. One of Remington's superior models is the **Micro Screen XLR810**. This razor produces a quality shave and comes equipped with an excellent trimmer.

The **BMS 7600** is another highly regarded Remington product. This razor, which is especially designed for the shaving needs of black men, features a special "beard lifter" which takes care of ingrown hairs and tough whiskers. It is also available in the **BMS 7800** rechargeable model.

Lady Remington shavers for women include the corded **WER 4200** and the rechargeable **WER 6200**. Both of these razors are designed with women's needs in mind and easily handle longer hair and stubble.

# Miscellaneous

## Lamson & Goodnow

**Lamson & Goodnow** has been manufacturing high-quality knives in western Massachusetts since 1837. Lamson & Goodnow now uses high-carbon, non-staining steel for its knives and kitchen tools. In 1990 it introduced a line of top-notch barbecue tools, available in gift boxed sets.

☎ *800-872-6564 (Lamson & Goodnow)*

## Zippo Lighters

**Zippo Manufacturing Co.** of Bradford, Pa., has been making world-famous Zippo lighters for nearly 60 years.

George Blaisdell invented this lighter during the Depression year of 1932. Later, Zippos were spread around the world by U.S. soldiers during the Second World War. A few years ago, the 200 millionth Zippo was sold.

Today's Zippo lighters feature a flint wheel that is good for as many as 73,000 strikes, and a practically infinite variety of durable, attractive cases. There are brass, chrome, gold-plated, colored and pictorial cases. Its collector series features the presidents of the United States, Wild West heroes, the American Flag, the Desert Storm insignia and others.

Zippo lighters are durable, interesting all-American gifts that are suitable for just about anyone. Best of all, Zippo guarantees these lighters will "work always...or Zippo fixes them free."

Zippo also manufactures writing instruments, knives, greenskeepers, money clips, keyholders, keyrings and rules in its Bradford factory.

*A Zippo WWII commemorative lighter*

☎ *(814) 368-2736 (Zippo)*

# ★☆ 16 ☆★
# Toys and Games

*The Made in the U.S.A. Foundation would like to thank Debbie Wager, author of Good Toys: Parents' Guide to Toys and Games, for her pioneering research on this chapter in 1989.*

## The Industry

Toys are big business in the U.S. In 1990, Americans spent approximately $13.13 billion dollars on toys and games. (This figure does not include video games.) On any given day, there are 150,000 different items found on the shelves of the nation's toy stores. Unfortunately, approximately 70-75% of these toys are imported.

Since toy production is usually heavily labor-intensive, many U.S. companies have been attracted by cheap foreign labor and shifted production offshore. Some firms combine both domestic and overseas production, while others make different parts of a toy in several world locations and assemble them here. Nevertheless, about 42,600 Americans have jobs in the toy industry in the United States, with 70 percent of these in production.

## American-Made Toys & Games

American toys are some of the best. They are usually higher quality, more durable, non-fad type toys that children will cherish for years to come. Many of them are time-proven "classics" that bring adults and children together. In contrast, imported toys are often poor quality, mass produced toys that are heavily television advertised and popular for just a short while.

In many cases, U.S.-made toys are also more educational. Many imported toys are passive, non-thinking video games or other complex toys that do everything for the child. U.S. toys, on the other hand, tend to be either open-ended play toys that allow children to improvise and use their imagination (blocks and drawing toys, for example), active toys (balls and outdoor play equipment) or games, puzzles and books that involve thinking and decision making.

Thus, although all toys appeal to children and are fun for a while, U.S. toys are usually more durable, remain favorites for a longer period of time and generally inspire healthy, growthful play. Although in many cases, U.S. toys may be more expensive than imported ones, they are worth the extra cost. How many times have you had to replace or throw out your child's imported "bargain" because it broke or your child lost interest in a matter of weeks?

# Balls

## Koosh Balls

A Koosh Ball is named for the sound it makes when it hits your hand. It is a natural rubber ball that looks a lot like a porcupine that jiggles. Tactile, soft, bounceless and colorful, the Koosh ball is made with

*The joy of Koosh Balls*

custom, computer controlled machinery in which the rubber goes in one end, and 2,000 fingers of rubber filament Koosh ball comes out the other. The nature of a Koosh Ball makes it very safe and easy to catch—not too mention fun.

The Koosh ball was invented by Scott Stillinger, a computer company engineer, who became frustrated trying to teach his young children how to catch a ball. He and his brother-in-law, Mark Button, quit their jobs to start **Oddz On Products** and introduced the Koosh Ball in October 1987 in California. It flew off the shelves. In 1991, Koosh continues to be one of the top 20 non-television promoted toys in the country, Although some Koosh balls are now produced in China, around 90 percent are still made in Campbell, Calif.

## Nerf Products

In 1972, Parker Brothers introduced the **Nerf Football**, a 3/4 standard sized, dense foam rubber football that rapidly became the largest selling football in the world. Over the years, the Nerf line of "safe, soft, fun" products has grown to include **Nerf Soccerball, Turbo Nerf Football,** which is deeply ridged to allow it to be gripped easier and thrown further than a standard Nerf Football, and **Turbo Screamer Football,** which whistles as it sails through the air. Nerf also offers soft versions of just about any sport you can think of including **Pro Hoop** (basketball) and **Nerf Bow and Arrow.**

Nerf is currently owned by the Kenner division of **Hasbro Inc.** and manufactures its products in Salem, Mass. All Nerf products are designed to inspire children (and adults) to get out and be active while avoiding the injuries and damage that can occur with regulation balls and the passive play inherent in many other toys.

## Pinky Balls

Remember them from your childhood—those tennis ball-sized, wonderful pink-colored balls that bounced really well? Never fear, they are still made by Hedstrom, in Ashland, Ohio. At about a dollar a ball, you can't find more economical, American-made fun.

# Bubbles and Bubble Toys

**Strombecker Corp.'s** Chicago factory produces over 50 million bottles of **TootsieToy®**, **Mr. Bubbles** and **Wonder Bubbles** each year—making it the largest manufacturer of bubble products in the world. TootsieToy® bubble solution is not only loads of fun, but the safest bubble solution available. Many foreign brands are plagued by bacteria and other contamination problems.

Strombecker also makes various bubble toys in its plant in Durant, Okla., including **Mr. Bubble's Giant Wand** which can create eight-foot-long bubbles, **Mr. Bubbles Million Bubbles Wand**, and new in 1992—**Mr. Bubbles Bubble Sword**, which creates bubbles when pulled from its solution-filled scabbard.

# Dolls

## Middleton Collectible Dolls

**Middleton Doll Co.** has been making life-like, collectible, limited edition vinyl and porcelain dolls in Belpre, Ohio since 1978. Lee Middleton started sculpting dolls in the image of her own children in her kitchen in 1978. Today, Middleton dolls are at the top of collectors' demand lists. Lee is especially noted for her "babies."

Middleton Doll Co. is a family operation. The founder still works producing Middleton dolls, and her sister, Sharon Wells, designs some of the doll's clothing. As a result of Lee's deep beliefs, each doll comes with its own tiny Bible. Explains Lee, "It's our way of giving credit where the real credit is due."

Middleton dolls retail for $10-$500 and are available in specialty, gift and doll stores nationwide. Although the company will not ship directly to collectors, the company will direct customers to the nearest Lee dealer.

☎ *(614) 423-1717 (Middleton)*

# Collectible Horses

## Breyer Animal Creations

**Breyer Animal Creations,** a subsidiary of **Reeves International,** makes its hand-painted, finely detailed collectible horses in Wayne, N.J. Begun as a custom plastic molding company in 1943, Breyer made its first horse for a clock company, which commissioned it to adorn a timepiece. In 1950, Breyer went on to market its first horse, a Palomino, through F.W. Woolworth, and sales zoomed. Breyer has been producing high quality, hand-crafted models of equine legends ever since.

Breyer horses begin on a sculptor's table, where commissioned artists carve the horses out of clay. The sculptors define each detail, from the animals' muscle tone and bone structure to their proportionate size and overall shape. They are then cast in steel, injection molded of cellulose acetate plastic, and hand air-brushed to attain their realistic appearance.

Due to its loyal collector-base of 6- to 18-year-old girls, Breyer maintains close ties with youth horse activities, including 4-H, Riding for the Handicapped and the Camp Horsemanship Association. It also publishes the magazine *Just About Horses* five times a year.

Breyer Animal Creations are priced from $7 to $25 and are available in toy stores and tack shops nationwide. The only Bryer product that is not made in the U.S. is Breyer's miniature "Stable Mates."

## Colorforms

Colorforms are flexible, flat, vinyl shapes that children can easily arrange and stick to the sheets of vinyl-covered cardboard that comes with each set. They can be used again and again.

*A Colorforms "Play Shapes" set*

The first Colorforms set was created in 1951 by Harry Kislevitz in his apartment in the Bronx, N.Y. It consisted of basic geometric shapes in primary colors and cardboard dress- up dolls. Today, now world-famous Colorforms are manufactured in Ramsey, N.J., and features such characters as Ninja Turtles, Sesame Street and Disney characters and Waldo, not to mention different versions of the original Colorforms.

# Construction Toys

### Learning Materials Workshop

The **Learning Materials Workshop** carefully crafts a variety of award winning construction toys in Winooski, Vt. These construction toys emphasize color, design and creative thinking, and allow a child to use his or her imagination time and time again.

Learning Materials pieces are well-made and extremely durable. Every piece is crafted from the finest maple and birch hardwood, sanded and finished for beauty and smoothness and painted in bright (non-toxic) primary colors.

The pieces are also interchangeable so that their use grows along with the child.

One of Learning Materials' most popular toys is the **Playframe**, which includes pyramids, cubes, bobbins, beams, arches and other pieces, all on a 2' by 2' play surface. This toy received the 1990 Parent's Choice Award.

*The "Playframe" from Learning Materials Workshop*

Learning Materials toys average about $35 to $65, although the Playframe sells for $315.

☎ *(802) 862-8399 (Learning Materials Workshop)*

## Lincoln Logs

Lincoln Logs were invented by John Lloyd Wright, son of Frank Lloyd Wright, who got the idea while on a business trip to Tokyo with his father in 1916. As he watched workers move timbers into place for the Imperial Palace Hotel, he was inspired by the Japanese technique for constructing earthquake-proof buildings, and daydreamed of a toy that children could use to build little versions of the structures of America's past—such as log cabins, forts and bridges.

Wright worked out details for the toy upon his return to Wisconsin, and in 1918, he put Lincoln Logs on the market. The name was meant to invoke the spirit of Abraham Lincoln, but there wasn't much interest then. By the 1930s, it caught on, and children all over the country were building log cabins.

**Playskool,** a division of **Hasbro Inc.,** bought the rights to produce Lincoln Logs in 1943. Today, Playskool still uses Ponderosa Pine from national forests in Oregon to produce a variety of Lincoln Log sets in its factory in Walla Walla, Wash.

### Tinkertoys

Tinkertoy construction sets were introduced at the 1914 Toy Fair by inventor Charles Pajeau. From the beginning these novel toys attracted a great deal of attention. When a model was first displayed in a Grand Central Station window, it caused a tremendous traffic jam. Believe it or not, Lockheed once used Tinkertoys as a design model to build an airplane wing fuselage testing system.

Tinkertoy sets consist of a variety of spools and sticks which can be endlessly arranged and rearranged to build whatever a child imagines. Beginning in 1992, Tinkertoys will be made of plastic instead of wood. Tinkertoys are made by **Playskool** (Hasbro Inc.) in Pawtucket, R.I.

# Drawing Toys

### Crayola Crayons

Crayola Crayons have been made in Easton, Pa., since 1903, when the first box of eight different colored crayons was sold by **Binney & Smith Inc.** for five cents. Eighty-nine years later, over two billion Crayola Crayons are produced in Easton and plants in Canada, England and Mexico. Crayolas distributed in the U.S. are made in Easton. If you are unsure, check the back of the box for a Binney & Smith, Easton, Pa., marking.

Crayola Crayons still come in a box of eight crayons but are also available in boxes of 16, 24, 32, 48 and 64 crayons. Binney & Smith also offers large crayons for beginners, So

Big Crayons for the youngest artist, fluorescent, metallic and pastel colors, wipe-off crayons and anti-roll (flat sided) crayons. This year, Binney & Smith will introduce a parent's dream—washable crayons.

Binney & Smith also makes fine colored mechanical pencils, markers, paints, brushes, tools, modelling clay, art kits and coloring books—all manufactured in its second U.S. plant in Winfield, Kan.

## Etch A Sketch

Invented by Frenchman Arthur Grandjean, this world famous drawing toy has been manufactured by **Ohio Art Co.** since 1960. Designed to be a long lasting classic, Etch A Sketch allows children (and adults) to turn its knobs and "magically" create drawings.

The drawing takes place via a metal stylus that connects the two turning knobs. Depending on which knob or combination of knobs is turned, the stylus removes a powdered aluminum and plastic bead mixture from the glass window (covered with a protective mylar film) and "magically" draws horizontal, vertical or curved lines on the screen. When the box is shaken, the mixture recoats the screen and the lines disappear.

Ohio Art offers its well-loved classic red and gray models as well as small **Travel Etch A Sketch** and a **Mickey Mouse Etch A Sketch.** Although Ohio Art has a joint venture in Thailand that manufactures Etch A Sketch for the foreign market, the Bryan, Ohio, plant still continues to produce over 8,000 units every day, and all Etch A Sketches found in the U.S. are from this plant.

Ohio Art, which has been around since 1908, also still manufactures the metal tops, tea sets and drums it began during World War II, as well as a variety of other items, including **Making Creativity Fun** activity toys and **Michael Jordan Jammer** indoor basketball sets.

## Magic Slate

In the early 1920s, R.A. Watkins, the owner of a small printing plant in Illinois, was approached by a man who wanted to sell him the rights to a homemade device made of waxed cardboard and tissue on which messages could be printed and then easily erased by lifting up the tissue. Watkins wanted to think about it, and told the man to return the next day. In the middle of the night, the man called Watkins from jail and said that if Watkins would bail him out, he could have the rights to his device. Watins agreed and went on to acquire a U.S. patent as well as the international rights for the device, which he called Magic Slate.

The Magic Slate is a cardboard pad with an acetate sheet you write on and then lift to erase. It is reusable time and time again, and its compact nature makes it ideally suited to car trips or other places where a child cannot bring along other toys. Modern Magic Slate sets include cardboard backing sheets that feature such characters as Little Mermaid, Tiny Toons and Disney characters.

Magic Slates are made by **Western Publishing** in Racine, Wis., and Fayattesville, N.C.

## Fisher-Price Products

From its beginnings in 1930 in East Aurora, N.Y., **Fisher-Price** has become the largest manufacturer of infant and preschool toys in the world. Fisher-Price was first known for its pull-toys named Granny Doodle and Doctor Doodle. After years as a subsidiary of Quaker Oats, Fisher-Price is again an independent global producer best known for its brightly colored, durable plastic toys.

Despite its global production, including plants in England and Mexico and Chinese sourcing, Fisher-Price still makes some old, molded-plastic favorites in Medina, N.Y., and Murray, Ky., including **Rock-A-Stack, Snap Lock Beads, Cash Register, Little Snoopy Sniffer** and **Bubble Mower.**

*Fisher Price "Rack-a-Stack" (l) and "Bubble Mower" (r)*

# Games

## Milton Bradley

**Milton Bradley Co.** began as a lithography company in Springfield, Mass. When the company's best selling product, a picture of a clean-shaven Abraham Lincoln, fell drastically when Lincoln grew a beard, owner Milton Bradley created a game to keep his printing company in business. Bradley called it "The Checkered Game of Life" and made the board a checkerboard because he thought life was just that—checkered and uncertain. It sold 45,000 copies in 1860 and put Milton Bradley on the road to becoming the largest producer of games and puzzles in the world.

Today, Milton Bradley is owned by **Hasbro Inc.** and remains the world's largest producer of games and puzzles. The majority of its games are either completely made in its plant in East Longmeadow, Mass., or printed and assembled in Longmeadow but contain imported pieces such as dice or timers. (This is true of almost all board games "made in the U.S.A.")

Many classic and well-loved Milton Bradley games are still completely made in the U.S.A., including **Chutes and Ladders, Candyland, Memory, Connect Four, Perfection,**

**Barrel of Monkeys, The Game of Life, Scrabble,** and **The Game of the States.**

**The Game of Life** is the updated version of the original "The Checkered Game of Life." It was revived to celebrate the company's centennial in 1960. Ironically, each game reflects its times. "The Checkered Game of Life" was a morality play—the object of the game was a happy old age, with right and virtuous choices advancing a player toward that goal. In contrast, in "The Game of Life" you choose to go to college or engage in business, and the object is to become a millionaire.

**Scrabble** is the second all-time top-selling board game in America. It was invented in 1931 by Alfred Butts to occupy his days of unemployment during the Great Depression. In 1948, a family friend finally convinced Butts that the game had commercial value and persuaded him to copyright it. Originally called "Criss Cross Words", Scrabble players pick letters on wood tiles (made in Vermont) and form words on a large crossword puzzle. An estimated two million Scrabble games are sold each year—including French, German, Hebrew, Italian, Russian, Spanish and Braille versions.

**The Game of the States** is a particularly fascinating game for families interested in products made in the U.S.A. The game consists of driving a car across the U.S. and buying and selling products each state is known for—such as Kansas wheat and Detroit cars.

Two new Milton Bradley games that are 100% made in the U.S.A. are **Splat!**, in which children try to get clay bugs to the kitchen for a midnight snack without being squashed by their opponents, and the wildly popular **NASCAR® Daytona 500® Race Game.**

Some classic Milton Bradley games that are printed and assembled in the U.S. but include an imported part such as the timer, buzzer, spinner or die are **Cootie, Twister, Scattegories** and **Taboo.**

Since 1990, the boxes for these games, as well as all other Milton Bradley games and puzzles, are made from 95%

recycled post-consumer waste (as opposed to factory clippings, which Milton Bradley has recycled since 1971).

## Monopoly

Monopoly is sold by **Parker Brothers,** another division of Hasbro Inc. However, this classic game is actually manufactured at Milton Bradley's East Long Meadow, Mass., plant. Monopoly is the world's best selling board game and has been translated into 23 different languages. This classic all-American game, which was invented during the Great Depression, uses the streets of Atlantic City, N.J., as the properties opponents buy and sell. As with many board games, Monopoly tokens and dice are imported.

## Intempo Toys

**Intempo Toys** manufactures 100% of its board games and puzzles in Los Angeles, Calif. and Holyoke, Mass. Intempo Toys specializes in games that help children understand and learn to love art and music.

The company was founded in 1987 by a former art teacher and a lawyer who could not find toys that would help them introduce their own children to the fine arts.

*Intempo's "In the Picture"*

One of Intempo's most popular games is **In the Picture** which has children search a museum for art clues to solve the mystery of a missing painting—either a child's re-creation of a famous work of art or a print of a famous piece. This game has won many awards including the 1991 Parent's Choice Gold Award and ranking in the Chicago Tribune's top five children's games of that same year. Intempo games are reasonably priced at $14-$20 and can be found in specialty toy stores and bookstores.

☎ *(800) 362-TOYS (Intempo)*

## Lionel Trains

Electric trains were first developed by Mario Caruso, an Italian immigrant who took the primitive battery-powered "box on tracks" invented by Lionel Cowan and fashioned it into a realistic model train. **Lionel Trains Inc.** began making electric trains in 1900.

After decades of tremendous success and growth in which Lionel became the best loved name in electric trains, the company fell on hard times and a series of corporate takeovers in the 1980s. At one point, train production was moved to Tijuana, Mexico, with disastrous results. The new plant could not maintain the quality expected of Lionel and often missed delivery dates, which further irritated retailers. It also vexed model railroad hobbyists like Richard P. Kughn, a Detroit investor who led a group of investors in buying Lionel. After becoming chairman and CEO, Kughn immediately insisted on moving manufacturing back to its prior base in Mount Clemens, Mich. Kughn rehired many of the plant's former workers, reemphasized product quality and spread the word among enthusiasts that Lionel was back on track.

Since Kughn's takeover, Lionel has broadened its product line, become the dominate producer of a wide array of classic and collectable trains and tripled its sales volume. Today, Lionel is back to producing world renowned, high quality train sets for children and limited edition trains and accessories for hobbyists and adults.

Each Lionel train combines the best of modern technology with traditional handmade craftsmanship. Aside from its classic offerings, Lionel is continually developing new electric train products—including those featuring Disney characters.

*Lionel's 027 gauge Mickey Mouse World Tour Train*

Lionel train sets, cars and accessories can be found at toy and hobby shops nationwide. Although over 90% of Lionel products are made in Michigan, a few accessories and single cars are made offshore. The packages on these items will read "made and lithographed in Korea," etc.

☎ *(313) 949-4100 (Lionel)*

# Large Molded Plastic Activity Toys

## Little Tikes

Little Tikes toys are all made in the U.S.A. in Hudson, Ohio. As founder and former president Tom Murdough Jr. said, "We wouldn't have it any other way."

Little Tikes was founded in 1970 by Murdough, with nine employees and one rotational molding machine with the idea of producing colorful, durable, plastic play things in a "do it right" atmosphere.

*Little Tikes Cozy Coupe*

Since 1984, Little Tikes has been a subsidiary of Rubbermaid and is currently the largest rotational molder of plastic in the world.

Little Tikes toys, which are designed for preschoolers, are noted for their clean design, durability and overall quality. One Little Tikes toy that has won repeated praise is **Little Tikes Place**, a doll house furnished with a family of durable, well-built little people, including black and Asian families. Some of its most popular toys are **Tap-A-Tune Piano**, **Cozy Coupe Car**, **Turtle Sandbox**, **Party Kitchen** and **Activity Gym**.

Little Tikes has a strong commitment to customer service. It was the first American toy manufacturer to mold its toll-free number into every product in 1983, and it has over 45 people on its customer service staff, which receives over 400,000 calls a year.

☎ *(800) 321-0183 (Little Tikes)*

*Little Tikes Activity Gym*

## Today's Kids

**Today's Kids** makes all of its large molded plastic toys in Booneville, Ark. The company used to be called Wolverine

Toy company and made metal toy kitchen appliances, tea sets and dishes. In 1986, it switched to colorful, molded plastic for several new toys and changed its name to Today's Kids. The new toys were very popular and the company began specializing in colorful, bulky, plastic activity toys for playschoolers.

The most popular Today's Kids items are **All-Star-Basketball, Kid's Workbench, Kid's Kitchen, The Merry Go Round** and the multi-activity **Toddler Playground.** This large toy has a number of activities, including crawl-through areas, a slide, steps, a shape sorter, a xylophone, a telephone and a ball chute.

One of Today's Kids newest products is the **390 Activity Rocker,** which is a little rocker with a console full of busy activities. It is designed to be a child's first situp toy.

Every Today's Kids toy has a three-year "Kid Tough" guarantee.

*The new 390 Activity Rocker by Today's Kids*

☎ *(800) 258-TOYS (Today's Kids )*

# Play-Doh

**Play-Doh** was introduced by Kenner Toys in 1955 and is one of the company's oldest and most successful toy lines. Play-Doh is a non-toxic modelling compound that is colorful, soft and easily shaped and reshaped time and time again. Although originally available only in white, by 1957 Play-Doh was available in eight standard colors. As of 1992, Play-Doh will include neon colors sets.

Besides the basic **Case of Colors,** Play-Doh offers a variety of playsets that include gadgets and molds for Play-Doh.

Two of the best and most popular playsets are **Make A Meal,** which includes rolling pins and a spaghetti making machine and **Hairdo Dolly** which lets a youngster grow the doll's hair, cut it and begin again.

Play-Doh and Play-Doh Playsets are manufactured in Cincinnati, Ohio by **Playskool,** a division of Hasbro.

# Puzzles

## Big Ben

**Big Ben Puzzles** is 50 years old in 1992. These classic 1,000-piece puzzles, which are designed for adults, are made by Milton Bradley (Hasbro) in East Longmeadow, Mass. Milton Bradley also makes a variety of other quality puzzles for both children and adults in this Massachusetts plant.

## Intempo

**Intempo Toys** of Palo Alto, Calif., is the only U.S. company that produces fine art puzzles designed for children. The puzzles feature reproductions of famous works by artists such as Van Gogh, Renoir and Miro. The number of puzzle pieces ranges from 80 for smaller children to 100 and 500 for older children. (Other information on Intempo Toys can be found in the Games section of this chapter.)

☎ *(800) 362-TOYS (Intempo)*

## Lauri

**Lauri** has been making outstanding crepe foam rubber puzzles since 1960. Lauri makes over 150 products for children 2 to 10 years old, including puzzles, alphabets, numbers, lacing and stringing activities and construction sets—all made in the U.S. in Phillips-Avon, Maine.

Lauri puzzles and manipulation sets have won many awards of excellence. Lauri perception puzzles are particularly good and are praised for their quality design. These perception puzzles show groupings of animals, cars and people, each one slightly different from the others in size, type or action. Children must perceive the subtle differences to fit in the pieces.

*Chubby and Large Pattern crepe foam puzzles by Lauri*

Lauri's crepe foam rubber pieces are washable and bendable, but they won't curl, crease or tear, and the color doesn't fade. Children love the texture, and if a piece is lost, the consumer can get a replacement for a 50-cent handling fee. Lauri's Playmill also makes a line of wooden puzzles and activity sets.

Lauri and Lauri's Playmill products are very reasonably priced and can be found in gift and specialty stores nationwide.

☎ *(207) 639-3555 (Lauri)*

# Radio-Controlled Toys

## Cox

**Cox** is the only manufacturer of radio-controlled products made in the U.S.A. For younger children, Cox makes line control planes, which have a small line attached from the plane to the handle. Cox also makes free flight helicopters, a free flight flying saucer, preassembled rockets that use Estes engines, and gas and electric powered fail-safe planes.

☎ *(800) 451-0339 (Cox)*

# Rocketry

Rocketry is as American as Disneyland. In 1958, soon after the first Sputnik was launched, **Estes Model Rocket Co.** lifted off in Penrose, Colo. Estes, which has been owned by **TCW Trust Co.** of the West since 1990, makes working rocket models that can go more than 1,000 feet in the air. Children enjoy building and painting the rockets as much as the launch itself.

Estes rockets are reusable and are available as simple models or as part of starter kits that include the launcher and rockets necessary for launches. Modern Estes products include models of the Patriot Missile, SDI Satellite, SR71 Blackbird and the Phoenix.

☎ *(719) 372-6565 (Estes)*

## Silly Putty

Silly Putty was developed accidentally in a General Electric laboratory during World War II, where scientists were trying to develop an inexpensive synthetic rubber substitute to make Jeep and airplane tires, tank treads and G.I. boots. Company engineer James Wright worked with boric acid and silicone oil and created a rubber-like compound with highly unusual properties. The pink substance could stretch like taffy, bounce off walls like a ball and, when struck with a hammer, shatter like glass. Although it became a novelty and curiosity on the cocktail party circuit, the scientists had no use for it.

After seeing the putty at a cocktail party, a Connecticut marketing man by the name of Peter Hodgson bought the rights to it. He packaged half-ounce dabs of the stuff in plastic egg-shaped containers and sold millions each year. People used it to take lint off clothes, clean typewriter keys, level wobbly furniture, and plug leaks. When Hodgson died in 1976, he left an estate of $140 million.

**Binney & Smith** (the Crayola people) bought the rights to Silly Putty in 1977 and have been manufacturing it in Easton, Pa. ever since. Binney & Smith sold 6 million eggs of Silly Putty in 1991 alone.

New uses for silly putty are found all the time. Athletes squeeze it to strengthen their hand muscles, while Apollo 8 astronauts used it during the space flights to fasten their tools during weightlessness. Many people are now hailing Silly Putty as a great tool for stress relief. Busy executives and others keep a wad handy on their desk and squeeze and reform it when things get hectic.

# Sleds

**Flexible Flyer**, the world's most famous sled, turned 100 years old in 1989. This enduring wooden sled, instantly recognizable by its Red Eagle trademark, was invented in 1889 by Samuel Leeds Allen of Philadelphia, a brilliant Quaker businessman who manufactured farm equipment. Afraid that his workers would take jobs on nearby farms during the slow winter season, Allen began work on a new product. With a passion for sledding ("coasting" in those days) and a love of invention, Allen eventually developed and patented a sled that revolutionized the sport. He replaced wooden runners with flexible, T-shaped, steel ones, then fixed the front with a movable, steerable cross-bar, added a slatted seat and named it the "Flexible Flyer."

The sled was hardly an overnight success. His salesmen did not like selling it, since the sales season cut their vacations short. Department store buyers were wary of this new "impractical" invention. However, by the early 1900s, with a revival of interest in such outdoor sports as golf, skating and tobogganing—the Flexible Flyer began its climb to fame.

Today, Flexible Flyer is owned by **Par Industries** and Flexible Flyer sleds are produced in West Point, Mich. Although the classic wooden Flexible Flyer is still churned out at about 150,000 sleds a year, Flexible Flyer also manufacturers over a million plastic sleds, including saucers and toboggans.

## Slinky

Richard James was a marine engineer aboard ship in 1943 when a coiled, circular torsion spring, fell off a table and began rolling around the deck. Its wild gyrations amused him and he thought it would make a great toy. James started tinkering with various metals, thicknesses and proportions of metals, and two years later, he perfected a coiled, steel spring that could spiral from one spot to another and "walk" down stairs. His wife Betty went to the dictionary, and found the name "Slinky." The Jameses persuaded the Gimbles store in Philadelphia to allow them to set up a sloped board in the toy department, where "Slinky" could walk. Within 90 minutes, all 400 in stock were sold.

In 1945, they set up **James Industries** in Hollidaysburg, Pa., which continues to manufacture Slinky products under the watchful eye of Betty James. In the 1990s, the Slinky line includes a Slinky Junior, two-color Plastic Slinkys, and Slinky Eyeballs. However, the original Slinky still outsells the others.

# Stuffed Animals

Most stuffed animals are imported. It is very difficult to find a domestically manufactured stuffed toy in the U.S. today. However, we have found three companies that produce quality stuffed toys here in the U.S.

*Papa, Mama and Baby Rabbit by Country Critter*

*Raggedy Ann and Andy dolls and stuffed blocks by the Toy Works*

*Ethan & Fanny Allen by the Vermont Teddy Bear Co.*

## Country Critter

**Country Critter** puppets and stuffed animals are made in Burlington, Kan. Country Critter, established in 1980, is one of the largest puppet makers in the world. Its puppets and stuffed animals are extremely life-like animals, including pigs, cows, bears, rabbits and more exotic animals. Country Critter also manufactures a variety of "Ride-On Toys," which are large plush animal toys designed for sitting, romping, or riding on, and pocket-sized stuffed animals called **Cottage Critters**. Country Critter stuffed toys and puppets can be found in toy stores and Hallmark and other gift stores nationwide.

☎ *(800) 444-9648 (Critters)*

## TheToy Works Silk Screen Dolls

**The Toy Works** manufactures silk screen dolls, blocks and other stuffed toys based on characters from classic children's literature.

The company began just 17 years ago when founder John Gunther tried to reproduce a silk screen "Tabby Cat" he saw in the Museum of the City of New York. Gunther perfected the reproduction process and The Toy Works is now considered the world's best silk screen printer of antique rag doll reproductions.

The Toy Works reproductions are vividly life-like—they seem to have stepped off the pages of your favorite children's book—and include such characters as Tabby Cat, Punch and Judy, Pug Dog, Rooster and the Seven Little Kittens. All Toy Works creations are manufactured in Middle Falls, N.Y. They cost between $9 and $50 and can be found at gift, specialty, museum and department stores nationwide.

☎ *(800) 237-9566 (Toy Works)*

## Vermont Teddy Bear Company

**Vermont Teddy Bear Co.** makes high-quality stuffed teddy bears (and an occasional seasonal bunny rabbit) in its factory in Williston, Vt. The bears come in four different sizes and four different colors and can be accessorized with a variety of clothing. Gift "BearGrams" are also available. Customers can also request a "Teddy Bear Gazette" that illustrates and gives ordering information on VTBC bears, or discuss possible bear choices with a telephone "Bear Counselor."

Since VTBC bears are made from Wisconsin fur, North Carolina stuffing and eyes from New York, whatever you choose, you will receive a 100% made in the U.S teddy bear.

☎ *(800) 829-BEAR (Vt. Teddy Bear)*

## Swingsets

Each year, **Creative Playthings** manufactures tens of thousands of wooden swing sets, making it the largest manufacturer of wooden backyard playground equipment in the country. The swing sets are well-built and made to last —each one carries a 25-year warranty. The swing sets are made in Herndon, Pa., and retail from $499 and up. Although the sets are unassembled, most stores (including Sears and Toys "R" Us) provide delivery and installation services.

## Tonka Trucks

**Tonka Corp.** was founded in 1946 in the basement of a small schoolhouse near Lake Minnetonka, Minn. After acquiring both Kenner and Parker Toys and becoming one of the country's largest toy manufacturers, Tonka was bought by **Hasbro Inc.** in 1991. Although some Tonka trucks are now made offshore, the majority of are made in El Paso, Texas.

Texas-made Tonka trucks include: **Tonka Mightys,** which are lifetime-guaranteed, large all-steel construction type trucks; **Tonka Large Steel** trucks, which are smaller 4 by 4s, pickups and "monster trucks" made of steel and plastic; and **Tonka Large PreSchool** vehicles, which are all-plastic, lifetime-guaranteed, furniture friendly vehicles, including fire trucks, garbage trucks and schoolbuses.

U.S.-made Tonka trucks sell for $10 to $90 and can be found in toy stores across the country. Remember, not all Tonkas are U.S. made, so check the box.

# Wagons and Other Ride-On Toys

### Roadmaster

**Roadmaster Corp.** makes bright red, classic metal and wood wagons in Olney, Ill. The Olney factory also manufactures a variety of sturdy metal and plastic ride-on toys that are pedal-driven vehicles for 2- to 6- year olds. Roadmaster's ride-on toys include a tractor, a fire truck, jeeps and trucks. These Roadmaster toys can be found in toy stores, Kmart and other retail chains. Roadmaster tricycles and children's bicycles are discussed in the Bicycle chapter.

*A Roadmaster wagon*

# Yo-Yo

The yo-yo had its origin as a primitive weapon in the Philippine Islands long before there was a printed word. It was fashioned from a sharp piece of flint-like rock with a long thong tied to it. If a native's aim was poor, at least the hunter could retrieve the weapon, and the hunting expedition wouldn't be a total loss! During the 17th and 18th centuries, the yo-yo evolved into a favorite diversion in the royal courts of Spain and France.

Duncan Toys introduced this toy to the United States in the 1920s, where it officially became known as the Yo-Yo. **Duncan Toys**, a division of **Flambeau Products**, still makes the majority of its famous Yo-Yos in the U.S. in Columbus, Ind. All Duncan Yo-Yos are currently made from plastic and include such well-loved models as the Butterfly, Imperial and Midnight Special. To find a particular Duncan Yo-Yo call the number below. And remember,"If it's not a Duncan, it's not a Yo-Yo."

☎ *(800) 356-8396 (Duncan)*

# ★☆ 17 ☆★
# Tools

Nowhere is the superiority of American craftsmanship more evident than in the design and manufacture of electric and hand tools. Anyone, from the beginning do-it-yourselfer to the master craftsman, can find quality tools made in the U.S.A.

## Hand Tools

### American Tool

American Tool Co. manufactures all of its excellent hand tools in the United States, mostly in Lincoln, Neb. American Tool offers **Vise-Grip** locking pliers and specialty locking tools, **Quick-Grip** one-handed bar clamps, **Unibit** step drills, **Prosnip** tin and aviation snips and **Chesco** hex key sets. All of these tools pass a rigid factory inspection and carry a full warranty against defects in materials and workmanship.

☎ *(402) 683-5800 (American Tool)*

### Channellock

**Channellock** was started over 100 years ago by George DeArment in Conneaut Lake, Pa. This company's tongue and groove adjustable pliers, invented in 1933, evolved into a wide assortment of pliers, snips, electricians' knives, wire cutting and crimping tools, adjustable wrenches and ball peen hammers—all of which are still made in the USA.

## Craftsman

Sears offers an excellent line of hand tools under the Craftsman label. These tools are all American-made and backed by an unconditional lifetime warranty—if a Craftsman tool ever breaks, it will be replaced free of charge.

In contrast to Craftsman tools, Sears' regular hand tools are generally lower-quality, imported tools.

## Estwing

Estwing produces all of its top quality hammers, hatchets, picks and prybars in the U.S.

## Stanley

When one thinks of American hand tools, one thinks of Stanley. This American company, which was founded in 1843, currently produces over 2,000 tools and related products—the vast majority of which are still made in the U.S. in Covington, Ga.

## Vaughn

Vaughn is another U.S. manufacturer of all American-made top-quality hammers, picks, hatchets and prybars.

# Power Tools and Accessories

## Dewalt

Dewalt is the new name for Black & Decker's professional line of power tools. These top of the line tools are all made in the U.S.

To complement its premium Dewalt tools, **Black & Decker** also offers a full line of American-made saws, sanders, drills and routers for the do it yourselfer. These are quality tools at a reasonable price. (*Note:* Black & Decker's ELU woodworking tools are manufactured abroad.)

## Craftsman

Black & Decker power tools are sold by Sears under its **Craftsman** label.

## Hirsh

For securing your project, **Hirsh** offers a variety of workstations, saw horses, tool stands, stools and adjustable work supports.

## Milwaukee

Ninety-five percent of **Milwaukee**'s line of electric and cordless tools are manufactured in their plants in Wisconsin, Alabama and Mississippi. Milwaukee tools are for the professional who requires performance and durability.

For example, the Milwaukee 7 1/4" contractor's saw ($150) features heavy-duty construction, all ball and roller bearings and excellent balance—and weighs just 11.5 lbs.

*Milwaukee's heavy-duty Magnum drill*

## Porter-Cable

**Porter-Cable** produces a wide range of U.S.-made electric tools. Its power sanding equipment is considered by many to be the best in the world. Belt sander models range from $150 to $360. The finishing sander, **Model 505**, is available for under $150. This heavy duty sander has precision balance and a high-speed orbit that allows the user to remove stock with less fatigue.

## Shopsmith

**Shopsmith** produces a single-unit complete home workshop in Dayton, Ohio. The Shopsmith home workshop includes a table, lathe, sander and drill press. Prices start at around $1500.

☎ *(513) 898- 9325 (Shopsmith)*

## Wagner

**Wagner** offers a variety of Minneapolis-made painting equipment. The **Powerscraper** removes old paint, while the **Powerpaint** applies paint with an airless spray system for both indoor and outdoor use. The **Powerroller** can siphon paint directly from the can, eliminating the paint tray and cutting your work time considerably.

## Wen

**Wen** makes all of its durable power tools in Indiana.

## Vermont American

Consider **Vermont American** for replacement blades, bits and drills. This company operates 19 plants in the United States, although a few of their specialized circular saw blades are manufactured in Canada and Australia.

# Accessories

## Tool Boxes

**Plano, Flambeau** and **Akro** all produce a variety of quality plastic tool, tote and utility boxes in the United States.

## Padlocks

There are two very good brands of American locks for keeping your tool box or other shop items secure: **Master Lock Co.** of Milwaukee, Wis., which is the world's largest manufacturer of padlocks, and **American Lock Co.** These two companies are the top selling locks in the United States. Most other kinds of padlocks are imported.

## Flashlights

Cheap imported flashlights are often poor quality and unreliable. Both **Brinkmann** and **Maglite** offer state-of-the-art aluminum flashlights that have adjustable beams, waterproof casing and unsurpassed records of reliability.

*Brinkmann flashlights*

# Lawn Mowers

Although imported lawn mowers are making inroads into the American market, many U.S. brands are equal in performance and more attractive in price. The following companies manufacture U.S.-made quality lawn mowers and lawn care tools.

| | |
|---|---|
| **Ariens** | **Sears** |
| **Cub Cadet** | **Snapper** |
| **Jacobson** | **Lawnboy** |
| **Toro** | |

*A Toro Recycler*

# ★☆ 18 ☆★
# Musical Instruments

## The Industry

Domestic market share in this industry has declined significantly over the past two decades. This has largely been the result of an infusion of cheap, mass produced imported instruments. Although American companies have largely lost the low end of this market, they have retained an internationally respected reputation for producing some of the world's finest high-quality instruments.

## Pianos

### Steinway

**Steinway & Sons** was founded in New York City by German immigrant Heinrich Steinweg, who changed his name to Steinway upon moving to America. Modern Steinways are hand-built in Long Island City, N.Y., for North and South America and in Hamburg, Germany, for European and Asian markets.

Since the company's inception in 1853, the name Steinway has been synonymous with the highest attainable level of quality and innovation. Steinway was instrumental in the evolution of the modern piano—acquiring approximately 133 patents throughout its history. Some of the major innovations Steinway is responsible for include the introduction of the overstrung grand piano, an improved keyboard action and the invention of the double cupola iron frame. All modern pianos are built with some "Steinway System" innovations.

Each Steinway piano is painstakingly handcrafted over the course of nearly two years. The highly skilled craftsmen of the New York factory, many of whom represent the second or third generation to work at Steinway, create approximately 2,500 pianos each year. This small production, which pales in comparison to mass market manufacturers that churn out as many as 200,000 pianos a year, is a testament to Steinway's attention to detail and complete devotion to hand-built quality.

For further evidence of Steinway quality, one need only examine the concert halls of the world where Steinways take center stage: Steinway pianos are the exclusive choice of over 90% of the world's performing artists.

As one would expect, Steinway pianos are quite expensive. A Steinway upright piano costs around $10,000, while Steinway grand pianos, to which the company devotes much of its production, retail for between $22,000 and $65,000.

*A Steinway grand piano*

## Mason & Hamlin Companies

In 1989, the Falcone Piano Company aquired the historic U.S. piano manufacturers Mason & Hamlin and Sohmer, and changed the company name to Mason and Hamlin Companies. The Mason and Hamlin Companies continue to produced distinct pianos under the **Mason and Hamlin, Sohmer** and **Falcone** names. All of them are made in the U.S.

## Mason and Hamlin

Mason and Hamlin pianos were first introduced in Boston in the early 1900s. These first pianos played to rave reviews and were quickly dubbed "The Stradivarius of Pianos."

However, following the Depression and ownership by U.S. Piano, Mason and Hamlin pianos fell on increasingly hard times. Finally, in 1986, the first of what would be a string of modern owners declared bankruptcy and ceased Mason and Hamlin production entirely.

The current Mason and Hamlin pianos were reintroduced in 1990. These small production, hand-built pianos are near perfect recreations of their lusterous ancestors. The rebirth of these great, distinctive pianos is a result of the newly formed Mason and Hamlin Companies' decision to reject the common practice of placing a newly acquired name on generic imported pianos and instead meticulously recreate these formerly great American pianos in a new Haverhill, Mass., plant.

Some new additions to these otherwise faithful recreations are its Renner actions and German Kluge keyboards, which the company considers to be the best such parts available.

## Sohmer

Sohmer pianos were the original creation of founder Hugo Sohmer, who emigrated to America from Germany and began his piano company in New York in 1870.

Sohmer pianos are currently produced by the **Mason and Hamlin Companies** in Elysburg, Pa., and are hand-built to the same rigid standards of raw materials and workmanship set forth by the company's founder.

Sohmer is perhaps best known for its 46" vertical "performance pianos," which have a reputation for superb tonality and touch response that rivals the best small grand pianos. Indeed, the full range of sound from a 46" Sohmer Vertical results from a distribution of strings that exceeds 96% of the strings on the company's 5' grand. These excellent pianos are designed not only as premium instruments, but as fine piece of furniture as well, and are available in a variety of classic hand-finished cherry, mahogony, oak and walnut exteriors.

## Falcone

The Mason and Hamlin Companies craft a limited number of Falcone (pronounced fal-có-ni) grand pianos in Haverhill, Mass. These custom grand pianos, which are designed for performance, the serious student or as an heirloom investment, are often described as the "Stradivarius of Keyboards." These handcrafted instruments feature a unique, high tension scale that requires each harp (or plate) to be individually hand cast and precision finished. The result is a family of grands with a variety of unique personalities favored by many of the world's great concert pianists.

## Baldwin

The Baldwin company proudly claims, "More Americans buy Baldwin pianos than any other brand, domestic or foreign."

Baldwin's large selection of pianos include 36"-42" spinets, or vertical pianos, for the home, larger studio pianos, concert verticals and the largest Baldwin Classics. These vertical pianos, which make up about 90% of the company's business, are made in Arkansas and Mississippi. The company's small line of grand pianos is made in Korea.

Although Baldwin is a somewhat of a mass producer (approximately 35,000 pianos a year), the company retains a high degree of quality. Indeed, many piano experts consider the Baldwin spinet the best on the market. Baldwin pianos range from around $3,000 to $42,000. The best models for home or school use are the **Hamilton School** piano ($3,100) and the **Home Studio** model ($3,600), which is available in decorator styles.

Baldwin also manufactures a line of electronic keyboards that are competitive with imported Japanese keyboards.

## Walter

The family-run **Walter Piano Co.** is a relative newcomer to American piano manufacturing. The first Walter piano was introduced by company founder Charles R. Walter in 1975. Since then, Walter console and studio pianos have become well-known for their sound and superb blending of modern technology and traditional craftsmanship.

Although the company boasts that Walter pianos "reflect a continuing program of product research," these pianos still embody the personal touch of old world craftsmanship: Charles Walter developed the company's "W-48" scale using the computer facilities at the University of Notre Dame, yet all Walter pianos are personally inspected and signed by a member of the Walter family before being sent out.

This year, this young company, which manufactures all its pianos in Elkhart, Ind., will complement its top-end upright pianos with the introduction of the first Walter grand.

# Guitars

Foreign companies import large quanities of less expensive, mass produced moderate quality guitars into the U.S market. To compete, many U.S. companies use imported guitars or components in their low-end lines.

However, the world's top-quality guitars continue to be made by American companies in the U.S. In fact, many of the imports entering the U.S. are simply "copies" of American-made guitars. For instance, Japanese-made Ibanez guitars are copies of the legendary American-made Gibsons.

## Fender

Rock and roll, with the help of the modern electric guitar, revolutionized the music world. Both are purely American innovations. The modern electric guitar was, for all intents and purposes, invented by Leo Fender in 1948 when he introduced the first commercially produced solid body electric Spanish guitar. Prior to this, musicians used hollow body electric guitars, which created a great deal of unwanted feedback and couldn't produce much volume.

The initial **Broadcaster** (later renamed Telecaster) guitars were initially designed for country and western but became the starting place for the rock and roll guitar. These early guitars were followed by the **Precision Bass**, the **Jazz Bass** and the legendary **Stratocaster**—which was played by visionaries like Buddy Holly.

Together, these guitars remain the industry leaders and are the foundation of popular music worldwide. Many of the world's best rock artists prefer a Fender. Guitar legends Jimi Hendrix and Eric Clapton have slung Stratocasters throughout their careers. Hendrix, who owned and played over 100 Fenders, was a driving force behind a massive 1967 Stratocaster revival that continues today.

Most recently, Fender introduced the **Stevie Ray Vaughan Signature Series Stratocaster** as a special memorial to the late Texas blues master. This special Stratocaster was commissioned by Vaughan himself and includes all the features that made his instruments unique. The majority of Fender electric guitars are still made in the U.S. in Corona, Calif. These guitars sell for between $500 and $1500 and can be distinguished from imported Fenders by examing the label on the headstock of the guitar. Fender also makes a complete line of **Fender Amplifiers**, which are made in Lake Oswego, Ore.

*The Stevie Ray Vaughan Signature Series Stratocaster*

## Gibson

Gibson stands beside Fender as one of the greatest U.S. guitar manufacturers.

Gibson guitars were "born" in Kalamazoo, Mich. at the hands of founder Orville H. Gibson in the 1890's. In the beginning, Gibson carefully handcrafted each guitar and mandolin himself. By 1902, Gibson had formed a company and employed the first of what was to become generations of skilled craftsmen making world-acclaimed Gibson instruments.Today, although the company also sells inexpensive, imported **Epiphone** introductory guitars, all guitars bearing the **Gibson** name remain made in the U.S and the epitome of quality and craftsmanship.

In fact, Gibson currently manufactures an entire range of highly acclaimed American-made instruments: Gibson electric and "jazz" guitars from Nashville, Tenn., Gibson acoustic guitars, mandolins and banjos crafted in Bozeman, Mont., strings, amplifiers and pickups from Elgin, Ill., and

North Hollywood, Calif.-made keyboards. Gibson also makes Steinberger and Tobias American-made guitars and bases.

*A Gibson "Les Paul"*

## Martin

**C.F. Martin & Co.** was founded by C.F. Martin in 1833 and has been producing some of the world's top acoustic guitars evers since. The company has an unchallenged reputation for consistent quality, which makes this small, privately held company a music industry legend. Martin quality is so well known musicians joke that as long as you can say " Martin guitar," you can communicate in any language.

Martin currently produces three separate lines of guitars. Top-of-the-line Martins remain hand-made in the United States in Nazareth, Pa. and in heavy demand by musicians around the world. The most popular of these $1,500-$6,000 guitars is the the **Dreadnought**, or D-size guitar which is used in every style of acoustic music.

On the other hand, Martin's mid-range guitars, which are found in the Shenandoah series, are finished in the U.S. from components entirely imported from Japan. Martin's Sigma line, which contains economical guitars for beginners and intermediates, is manufactured in Korea.

## Paul Reed Smith

The Paul Reed Smith guitar company is a newcomer to the music scene. This company began building hand-made electric guitars in Annapolis, Md., about 12 years ago. However, it wasn't until Carlos Santana began playing this brand of electric guitar in the early 1990s that the company really took off.

Although the company continues to grow—the initial staff of three has grown to 100 employees and these guitars are now in high demand in both Europe and Japan—founder Paul Reed Smith continues to concentrate on quality. The small Annapolis plant turns out only 350-400 guitars a year. Every part of these custom instruments is hand-made in the Annapolis factory—and Smith inspects every outgoing guitar himself.

Now that Paul Reed Smith guitars have an established reputation among electric guitar musicians, the company is reaching out to a new group of musicians with the 1992 introduction of its first acoustic guitar.

# Banjos

Some say the banjo is America's only native instrument, and American banjo makers are still turning out the best. Unlike in the guitar industry, copies of American banjos hardly exist. Some of the best American banjo makers include:

**Bacon Deering** *(Calif.)*
**Flat Iron Mandolin and Banjo Co.** *(Mont.)*
**Gibson** *(Tenn.)*
**Bart Reiter** *(Minn.)*
**S.S. Stewart** *(Pa.)*
**Stelling** *(Va.)*
**Vega**

# Ensoniq Keyboards

Over 90% of the electronic keyboards sold in the United States are manufactured in Japan. In the early 1980s, the electronics industry was awaiting the emergence of a low-cost sampler keyboard from the most likely source—Japan. However, in 1984 **Ensoniq Corp.** surprised many by introducing the first production "sampler" keyboard. ("Samplers" use computer stored, recorded sounds instead of the digital recreations found on most low-end synthesizers.)

*The Ensoniq "EPS" Performance Sampler*

In creating an affordable keyboard, which sported state-of-the art technology, Ensoniq not only upset the normally Japanese-dominated consumer industry, but turned itself into a multimillion-dollar company that exports keyboards all over the world, including, ironically enough, to Japan.

Ensoniq keyboards include the standard **VFX** and **VFX SD** models, which are state-of-the-art digital keyboards with programmable synthesizers with reverb and a 24-track sequencer, and the **Ensoniq EPS Performance Sampler,** which is a complete workstation capable of both recording and mixing compositions.

Ensoniq keyboards are made in Malvern, Pa.

☎ *(215) 647-3930 (Ensoniq)*

# Haynes Flutes

The **Wm. S. Haynes Co.** hand-crafts its excellent flutes and piccolos in Boston, Mass.—as it has since 1888. Contemporary Haynes' artisans, under the tutelage of Lewis J.

Deveau, president and master flutemaker, strive to perpetuate the coveted heritage established by founder William Haynes.

The fact that Haynes is the instrument of choice for flutists throughout the world, including legendary artists like George Barrere and Jean-Pierre Rampal, is testament to the fact that Haynes flutes are indeed masterpieces of contemporary craftsmanship.

Haynes flutes and piccolos offer not only vibrant, vivid sound but extreme versatility. Haynes flutes and piccolos include the Deveau Scale, which offers even intonation through all three octaves, and a choice of the unique Deveau or traditional headjoints. Best of all, Haynes is committed to complete customer satisfaction and will gladly exchange or recut headjoints to suit individual musicians (for up to a year after purchase) and will readily customize the instrument to individual desires.

Such individual attention is an integral part of the Haynes philosophy. As President Deveau explains, "We deal with the individual...We are 'custom' flute makers."

# ★☆19 ☆★
# Televisions

## The Industry

U.S. manufacturers have lost the television market. Since Zenith closed the doors of its Springfield, Mo., plant in March 1992, there are no longer any U.S. companies producing televisions in the United States.

However, Zenith and many other companies continue to produce television components in the U.S., and there are several foreign corporations assembling and manufacturing televisions here:

### Goldstar

*U.S. Company:* Goldstar of America Inc.

*Owned By:* Goldstar Co. Ltd. – Seoul, South Korea.

*U.S. Assembly Site:* Huntsville, Ala.

*American Sets:* Most 20″ and larger **Goldstar** sets and some **Sears** and **Radio Shack** sets. *Note:* All small-screen sets (less than 20″) are assembled in Mexico.

*American Content:* Over 50%, including American-made tubes and cabinets. *Note:* Some cabinets are imported from Korea.

### JVC (Japan Victor Company)

*U.S. Company:* U.S. JVC Co.

*Owned By:* Victor Co. of Japan Ltd. — Tokyo, Japan.

*U.S. Assembly Site:* Elmwood Park, N.J.

*American Sets:* 26"-35" color sets.
*U.S. Content:* More than 50%.

## Kotobuki

*U.S. Company:* American Kotobuki Electronics Industries, Inc.
*Owned By:* Matsushita Electric Industrial Co. Ltd.— Osaka, Japan.
*U.S. Assembly site:* Vancouver, Wash.
*American Sets:* 13", 20" and 27" diagonal combination TV/VCRs sold under the **Panasonic** and **Quasar** labels.
*American Content:* Not available.

## Matsushita

*U.S. Company:* Matushita Electric Corp. of America
*Owned by:* Matsushita Electric Industrial Co. Ltd.—Osaka, Japan.
*U.S. Assembly Site:* Franklin Park, Ill.
*American Sets:* some 20", 25", 27" and 31" **Panasonic** and **Quasar** brand color TVs *Note:* Some models are also assembled in Canada and Mexico.
**U.S. Content:** Approximately 70%

## Mitsubishi

*U.S. Company:* Mitsubishi Electric America.
*Owned By:* Mitsubishi Electric—Tokyo, Japan.
*U.S. Assembly Sites:* Santa Ana, Calif., and Braselton, Ga.
*American Sets:* 40"-120" rear projection and "big screen" TVs; 26", 27", 31" and 35" color TVs.
*U.S. Content:* 20% for projection TVs; 50% for color TVs. (The company plans to increase U.S. content to 50% and 60% respectively within the next three years.)

## Orion

*U.S. Company:* Orion Electric America Inc.
*Owned by:* Orion Electric Co. Ltd.—Takefu City, Japan.
*U.S. Assembly Site:* Princeton, Ind.

*American Sets:* Most **Emerson Electric** televisions.
*Note:* Emerson chose not to reveal which of its sets were assembled in the U.S. by Orion and would not release any information regarding content.

## Philips
*U.S. Company:* Philips Consumer Electronics Co.
*Owned By:* Philips Electronics—Eindhoven, the Netherlands.
*U.S. Assembly Site:* Greenville, Tenn.
*American Sets:* **Magnavox** and **Philips** brand televisions.
*Note:* All 13", 19" and 20" sets are assembled in Mexico.
*U.S. Content:* 75%-85% U.S. content (including U.S.-manufactured tubes, plastic, wood and current boards).

## Sanyo
*U.S. Company:* Sanyo-Fischer U.S.A. Corp.
*Owned By:* Sanyo Electric Co.—Osaka, Japan.
*U.S. Assembly Site:* Forrest City, Ark.
*American Sets:* 20", 25" and 26" color sets.
*U.S. Content:* Tries to buy as much U.S. and specifically Arkansas components as possible.

## Sharp
*U.S. Company:* Sharp Electronics Corp.
*Owned By:* Sharp Corp.—Osaka, Japan.
*U.S. Assembly Site:* Memphis, Tenn.
*American Sets:* 20" and up color sets.
*U.S. Content:* Approximately 70%.

## Sony
*U.S. Company:* Sony Corp. of America.
*Owned by:* Sony Corp.—Tokyo, Japan.
*U.S. Assembly Site:* San Diego, Calif.
*American Sets:* 27" and 32" color sets.
*U.S. Content:* All of these models contain American-made tubes.

## Tatung

*U.S. Company:* Tatung Co. of America.
*Owned By:* Tatung Co.—Taipei, Taiwan.
*U.S. Assembly Site:* Long Beach, Calif.
*American Sets:* All 27" color sets.
*U.S. Content:* Over 50% including cabinet, tubes and packaging.

## Thomson

*U.S. Company:* Thomson Consumer Electronic Inc.
*Owned By:* Thomson Consumer Electronic—Paris, France.
*U.S. Assembly Site:* Bloomington, Ind.
*American Sets:* All **RCA** and **GE** television sets.
*U.S. Content:* Over 50%. Manufactures many of its own components in U.S. *Consumer Reports* top-rated 27" model 27230 contains 80% U.S. content.

## Toshiba

*U.S. Company:* Toshiba America Consumer Products Inc.
*Owned By:* Toshiba Corp.—Tokyo, Japan.
*U.S. Assembly Site:* Lebanon, Tenn.
*American Sets:* All sets larger than 13".
*U.S. Content:* Generally 50% including American-made tubes, although some sets are less than 50% U.S. content.

# ★☆ 20 ☆★

# Cars and Trucks

## Import or Domestic?

Does it matter whether you buy a U.S.-built car? You bet. The U.S. automotive industry is a huge part of the national economy. It accounts for 4.5 percent of the gross national product, 2 million jobs and more than one-fourth of all the rubber, lead, iron stampings, machine tools, glass and semiconductors sold in this country.

Unfortunately, foreign companies have steadily eroded U.S. manufacturers' share of this gigantic industry. Today, foreign manufacturers control almost one-third of the U.S. auto and truck market, while foreign cars and auto parts account for an astounding two-thirds of our international trade deficit.

Clearly, purchasing an American car is the single most important contribution consumers can make to the health of the U.S. economy.

But are there really "American" cars out there, and are they worth purchasing?

# American Cars:
# Reality vs. Myth

Some people would argue there is no longer such a thing as an American car. Or they would tell you that buying an American made car means making a sacrifice, or that foreign cars have it all over American models.

Some people couldn't be more wrong.

There are many cars designed and built in the U.S by American companies using American parts. And it is easy to find a domestic car that costs less and gets better gas mileage than a comparable Japanese model, yet is equivalent in performance and construction and safer in an accident.

American cars may lag in one measure of refinement or another, but often the differences are so subtle they shouldn't sway a rational decision. In fact, what really keeps many owners of Japanese cars out of American car showrooms is a lag between perception and reality. Although many car buyers readily assume they are getting a better deal by choosing a Japanese import, the statistics suggest otherwise.

A recent study by the Economic Strategy Institute, a Washington think tank, showed that from 1976 to 1990, "Average U.S. quality has improved over 300 percent as opposed to only 30 percent for Japan." And Michigan-based automotive consultant James Harbour recently calculated the quality difference between new Japanese and U.S.-nameplate vehicles at less than one-fourth of a defect per car.

The Economic Strategy Institute study showed that the numbers of American car buyers reporting problems has fallen dramatically from 1976 to 1990, while Japanese buyers' complaints have increased. "U.S. producers have more than doubled the fuel economy of their fleet," the study also noted, "while Japanese producers have let their ratings slip."

Foreign nameplate cars still lead in some categories. But the domestic manufacturers aren't always upset about it:

☐ The Highway Loss Data Institute cited the Nissan 300ZX, built in Japan, as having the highest insurance claims for theft among 88 1990 models surveyed. The same survey found the German Volkswagen four-door Jetta the most stolen car of all.

☐ Of 15 small cars tested by the National Highway Traffic Safety Administration, the Toyota Paseo, Tercel and Corolla were the only ones in which serious head injury to drivers was rated as possible following 35-mph frontal crash tests with dummies.

# What Is an "American" Car?

There seems to be an appetite for change among foreign car owners. A majority of foreign car owners surveyed nationwide by the *Detroit Free Press* in 1992 said they sometimes feel guilty about not driving American cars. But for these and many other Americans, it is not always easy to determine what is—or is not—an American car. In fact, the more one learns about the international nature of the automobile industry, the more confusing it all becomes. A survey conducted by the Made in the USA Foundation discovered many Americans are blissfully ignorant of the national origins of many cars.

Understandably from their perspective, foreign manufacturers haven't done much to help clear up the muddle. In fact, they seem to be exploiting it. "You might think it's easy to tell a domestic car from an imported one... until you look at the full picture," says a glossy brochure of the Association of International Automobile Manufacturers, a trade group composed mostly of Japanese manufacturers. The brochure points out that this is a world where Hondas are built in Ohio, the Pontiac Le Mans is built in South Korea and the Mazda Navajo is little more than a rebadged Ford Explorer—designed and built in the United States.

Those who wish to use federal government standards to help them separate the domestic cars from the imports are in for additional frustration. The best known such standard is the one used by the Environmental Protection Agency for the determination of Corporate Average Fuel Economy, or CAFE. The CAFE law requires that the fuel economy of all of a manufacturer's cars averages 27.5 miles per gallon, but it distinguishes between each manufacturer's foreign and domestic fleets. It defines cars with 75 percent of their value in U.S. or Canadian parts and labor as "domestic," while those with 25 percent or less are termed "foreign."

This definition can be very misleading, however. The CAFE law defines the Mercury Tracer as a domestic, even though it is assembled in Mexico, because with "domestic" parts and cheap assembly, it meets the test. Some U.S. companies create further confusion by using just enough foreign (usually Mexican) labor and parts to classify their less fuel-efficient models as "imports" and consequently reduce the fuel economy average of their domestic fleet. Ford classifies the less fuel-efficient Ford Crown Victoria and Mercury Grand Marquis as imports, even though they are designed and engineered in the U.S., by buying numerous components in Mexico and assembling these two cruisers in Canada.

But don't despair. It is possible to rationally determine which cars have a more meaningful American parentage than others. Consider the following factors:

## 1. Nameplate

Does the car have the nameplate of an American firm? That matters because even if the car was designed or assembled overseas, much of the profits will flow back into an American company and its dealer network.

## 2. Design and Engineering

Was the car designed and engineered in the United States? If so, much of the brain power that created the car resides in this country. Buying a car that was designed in the United States helps protect the sorts of creative and high tech jobs that will keep the United States competitive in the future.

## 3. Assembly

Was the vehicle assembled in the United States? Those who build cars are also important to the economy, and keeping manufacturing jobs in the United States has an important impact on our future.

The best way to determine if a car was assembled in the U.S. is to check the vehicle identification number, or VIN. This seventeen character combination is generally found on the dashboard or windshield pillar. If the first character is a "1" or a "4", the car was assembled in the United States. (If the first character is a "J," it was assembled in Japan, a "2" Canada and a "3" Mexico.)

## 4. Content

Were most of the vehicle's parts, in terms of total dollar value, made in the United States? Again, the manufacturing of car and truck parts can have a significant impact on our economy. And while it is true that no vehicle is 100 percent made of U.S. parts, there are many American models that have more than 90 percent U.S. content.

Each of these factors affects the U.S. economy. The best "American buy"—or one that will contribute the most to the growth of our economy—is a vehicle that meets all of these criteria. In other words, the ideal car or truck is sold by an American company and is designed, engineered and assembled in the U.S. from a high percentage of American parts.

Remember, do not assume that because a car or truck has a U.S. nameplate that it meet all of these criteria. Be especially careful regarding assembly. Many "American" cars are now assembled outside the U.S. Only three U.S. nameplates are exclusively assembled in the United States. These are Lincoln, Oldsmobile and Saturn. All other nameplates include some foreign assembly cars.

To help you easily identify these "American" models assembled outside the U.S., consult the following chart. However, be careful—some of these models also are assembled in the United States. To make absolutely sure you are getting a car that was assembled in the U.S., check the VIN discussed above.

# U.S. Nameplate Cars and Trucks Assembled in Other Countries

| Company | Model | Final Assembly Site |
|---------|-------|---------------------|
| Dodge | Caravan [1] | Windsor, Ontario - Cananda |
| Dodge | Colt | Mizushima, Japan |
| Dodge | Monaco | Bramalea, Ontario - Canada |
| Dodge | Shadow Convertible [2] | Toluca, Mexico |
| Dodge | Stealth | Nagoya, Japan |
| Plymouth | Colt | Mizushima, Japan |
| Plymouth | Colt VIsta | Okazaki, Japan |
| Plymouth | Voyager [3] | Windsor, Ontario - Canada |
| Chrysler | LeBaron Sedan [4] | Toluca, Mexico |
| Chrysler | LeBaron Coupe | (Some) Toluca, Mexico |
| Dodge Trucks | Ram Pickup-Club Cab Models | Lago Alberto, Mexico |
| Dodge Trucks | Ram Van and Caravan C/V [5] | Windsor, Ontario - Canada |
| Dodge Trucks | Ram Wagon | Windsor, Ontario - Canada |
| Dodge Trucks | Ram Charger | Lago Alberto, Mexico |
| Chevrolet | Crew Cab Pickup (CK) | (Some) Oshawa, Ontario - Canada |
| Chevrolet | Lumina [6] | Oshawa, Ontario - Canada |
| Geo | Metro | Kosai, Japan |
| Geo | Storm | Fujisawa, Japan |
| Geo | Tracker | Ingersoll, Ontario - Canada |
| Jeep | Wrangler | Brampton, Ontario - Canada |
| Eagle [7] | Premier | Bramalea, Ontario - Canada |
| Eagle | Summit Wagon | Okazaki, Japan |
| Eagle | Summit 3-Door | Mizushima, Japan |

| Company | Model | Final Assembly Site |
|---|---|---|
| Pontiac | LeMans | Inchon, South Korea |
| Ford | Crown Victoria | Ontario, Canada |
| Ford | Escort | (Some) Mexico |
| Ford | Festiva | Seoul, South Korea |
| Ford | Tempo | (Some) Oakville, Ontario - Canada |
| Ford Truck | F-Series | (Some) Oakville, Ontario - Canada |
| Mercury | Capri | Broadmeadows, Australia |
| Mercury | Grand Marquis | St. Thomas, Ontario - Canada |
| Mercury | Topaz | (Some) Oakville, Ontario - Canada |
| Mercury | Tracer | Hermosillo, Mexico |

Grand Caravans are built in St. Louis, Mo.
Other Dodge Shadow models are built in Sterling Heights, Mich.
Grand Voyagers are built in St. Louis, Mo.
LeBaron Base and LX are built in Newark, Del.
Extended Ram Van and Grand Caravan C/V models are built in St. Louis, Mo.
Lumina APV passenger and cargo minivans are built in Tarrytown, N.Y.
Eagle Talons are built by Mitsubishi in Normal, Ill.

# The Best All-American Cars and Trucks

So much for models to avoid. What should you buy? Using the four criteria discussed above and the recommendations of consumer and auto publications, we have come up with a list of cars and trucks that are not only as American as you can get, but attractive, reliable, durable, fun to drive and a good value.

Here then, by price categories, are 20 of the best all-American cars and six of the best trucks and vans the U.S. has to offer. A short discussion of foreign nameplate cars assembled in the U.S. follows.

## SATURN
CATEGORY: Economy coupe and sedan
BASE PRICE RANGE: $8,470-$12,845
ASSEMBLED IN: Spring Hill, Tenn.

*1992 Saturn SC*

Saturn was a $1 billion gamble when General Motors announced it as a strategy to win back buyers of fuel-efficient imports more than half a decade ago. Now it looks like GM may have hit the jackpot. Almost half of all Saturn buyers had formerly driven imports, and the car is earning a well-deserved, cult-like following.

Saturn is arguably the greatest automotive value in the United States—foreign or domestic. Available in coupe or four-door, Saturn features durable plastic body panels, a fuel-thrifty and responsive engine, a spacious interior and a low price. The attention to detail in interior trim and its ride and handling rival the best of the imports. In fact, in a recent comparison test with the Honda Civic, Suzuki Swift and Hyundai Elantra, *Popular Science* called the Saturn "logically the best package overall."

And for 1992, just its second year of existence, Saturn is better than ever, with lower engine noise levels, an optional driver's side air bag and optional leather interior trim. It will also be available soon in a small station wagon model.

## FORD ESCORT
CATEGORY: Economy coupe, sedan, wagon
BASE PRICE RANGE: $8,730-$12,308
ASSEMBLED IN: Wayne, Mich.

*1992 Ford Escort LX*

Like a faithful old dog, the Ford Escort remains among the most enduring of low-priced car lines. But the Escort is certainly no dog when it comes to taking care of its occupants.

*Consumer Reports* said the Escort has the "solid feel of a larger car"—high praise indeed, considering the source. The Escort has a standard economy base 1.9-liter fuel-injected engine that generates just 88 horsepower but can motivate the car with surprising ease.

Available in three body configurations—sedan, hatchback or station wagon—the Escort can also be had in GT or LX-E models. However, these models feature a Mazda-built 16-valve engine that improves performance dramatically, but significantly lessens the degree to which it is truly made in America.

Also be aware that while most Escorts are assembled in Michigan, some, notably many of the GT models and some of the sedans, are assembled in Mexico.

## FORD MUSTANG
CATEGORY: Sports coupe, convertible
BASE PRICE RANGE: $10,655-$15,683
ASSEMBLED IN: Dearborn, Mich.

*1992 Ford Mustang Convertible*

Sure, this design is a bit long in the tooth, but the Mustang remains an American classic that, when outfitted with the legendary five-liter V-8 engine, can outperform almost anything else on the road. That's especially true this year, with the V-8 pumped up to a whopping 225 horsepower.

Those who are more interested in profiling than performing can order a Mustang in a more sedate iteration, namely the 2.3-liter engine, which features half the cylinders—and less than half the horsepower–of its fire-breathing cousin.

The Mustang carries the family's good looks that originated with the Taurus–namely the cat-like look of the front and the crisp-yet-curvacious look of the rear.

## CHEVROLET BERETTA
CATEGORY: Compact sport coupe
BASE PRICE RANGE: $11,474-16,060
ASSEMBLED IN: Wilmington, Del.

*1992 Chevrolet Beretta*

This is a sporty coupe that does many things well. The Beretta has a smooth five-speed shifter and optional automatic transmission, a suspension system that provides for nimble handling, standard anti-lock brakes and a driver's air bag.

The biggest letdown of the Beretta used to be the bland look of its interior, a failing that was remedied in the 1991 model year. The Beretta also has a fine power steering package and room for five.

The Beretta is available in several versions, ranging from a base model, whose engine generates 110 horsepower up to the GTZ model, with its 180 horsepower, four-cylinder powerplant.

## DODGE SPIRIT/PLYMOUTH ACCLAIM
CATEGORY: Compact sedans
BASE PRICE: $11,955
ASSEMBLED IN: Newark, Del.

*1992 Dodge Spirit ES*

Boxy and uninspired though their designs may be, these are attractively priced options for a growing family on a tight budget. These Chrysler-built twins provide room for six.

The standard 2.5-liter engine will provide reasonable acceleration and wonderful highway gas mileage. But if you can afford to pay for more power, the optional 3-liter, V-6 mated to the four-speed automatic can make your driving more entertaining. Alas, this engine is built by Mitsubishi in Japan.

After absorbing that low initial sticker price, you can be forgiven for loading your car up with such options as power windows and seats and a high-zoot stereo system.

Those who still yearn for more bang, and have the bucks, should consider the Spirit R/T with a Lotus-modified turbocharged and intercooled four-cylinder that has 224 horsepower and can make a trip to the grocery store a memorable experience.

## OLDSMOBILE ACHIEVA
CATEGORY: Compact coupe and sedan
BASE PRICE RANGE: $12,000-$17,500
ASSEMBLED IN: Lansing, Mich.

*1992 Oldsmobile Achieva SC*

This is the kind of American car that makes import intenders forget why they meant to buy an import. It has crisply contemporary exterior styling and an interior that looks like it came straight out of an Acura. In fact, anyone considering an Acura Integra should probably stop by an Olds dealership to consider this alternative.

Available in coupe or four-door models, the Achieva features standard anti-lock brakes and an overhead cam four-cylinder engine. It can also be ordered with a 160 to 180 horsepower double overhead cam four, or a 160 horse V-6.

The car has its pros and cons, however. In its favor is a range of lusty engines that want to propel it quickly and all-independent suspension that holds the car on the road. But critics complain its four-cylinder engine is too noisy on hard acceleration. Nevertheless, the Achieva seems to be selling well in its debut year. It is worth a look.

## PONTIAC GRAND AM
CATEGORY: Compact sport coupe and sedan
BASE PRICE RANGE: $12,374-$14,274
ASSEMBLED IN: Lansing, Mich.

*1992 Pontiac Grand AM GT Coupe (front) and sedan (back)*

To their credit in an age of look-alike cars, Pontiac stylists take more chances than anyone else. Consider the Grand Am, which on the outside may look less like a car than an Origami class project. And the interior design is as swoopy and organic as a modern interpretation of Art Nouveau.

But the results are ergonomically correct. There's more room in the rear seats of this compact model, and the doors swing open wider on the four-door models.

Under the hood, your options include a variety of four-cylinder engines, cranking out from 120 to 180 horsepower, or a 160 horse V-6. In almost any configuration, this car is entertaining on the road, though its four-cylinder engine is known to get a little buzzy in hard acceleration.

## FORD TAURUS
CATEGORY: Mid-sized, four-door sedan
BASE PRICE RANGE: $15,470-$ 24,329
ASSEMBLED IN: Chicago, Ill.; Atlanta, Ga.

*1992 Ford Taurus*

For 1992, the Taurus, that workhorse of mid-sized cars, has been the subject of hundreds of refinements—from a retuned suspension for better handling to a redesign of the entire interior.

Now the dashboard sweeps around its occupants and features remote radio controls, larger door handles and bluish-tint interior lighting—found to be easier to cope with in night driving. The least obvious changes were made in exterior styling. After all, Ford reasoned, why fool around with a design that stunned the world when it was introduced in the early 1980s?

The car has grown 3.8 inches longer and has been updated just enough to remain contemporary. No longer can a Taurus be ordered with a four-cylinder engine. The minimum engine is a three liter V-6 with 140 horsepower, but you can opt all the way up to a wild, 220 horsepower V-6—though that engine, in the SHO, is engineered by Yamaha in Japan.

## OLDSMOBILE CUTLASS SUPREME
CATEGORY: Mid-sized coupe and four-door
BASE PRICE RANGE: $16,200-22,400
ASSEMBLED IN: Doraville, Ga.

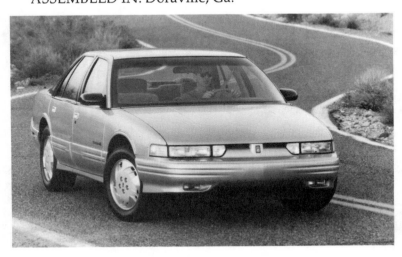

*1992 Oldsmobile Cutlass Supreme SL*

This is not supposed to be the kind of car an enthusiast could enjoy. Though nicely proportioned, it seems somehow too sedate—unless you order the car with GM's surprising twin dual cam V-6.

The twin cam is an engine that likes to sing as it works. The twin cam will pull you along with impressive power, yet it delivers good fuel economy and doesn't mind if you fill the tank with regular unleaded gas.

Available in coupe and four-door version, the Cutlass can also be ordered with one of GM's more unique options, head-up display, which allows the driver to have information from gauges projected on the windshield, much the way a fighter pilot does.

## FORD THUNDERBIRD
CATEGORY: Full-sized sports coupe
BASE PRICE RANGE: $16,840-$22,541
ASSEMBLED IN: Lorain, Ohio

*1992 Ford Thunderbird LX*

For those whose tastes tend toward the sporty, but whose budget and practical considerations dictate something capable of accommodating a family, the Thunderbird, of all models, may provide an entertaining solution.

This is one of those cars that really could get by on looks alone. It doesn't just sit on the road, it seems to hunker. Its aggressive facade features two flared, bumper-mounted air intakes. Yet the interior offers generous back-seat room, and the trunk can handle a surprising amount of gear.

Once under way, the Thunderbird really displays its charms, to the driver, particularly if he or she passes up the standard 140 horsepower V-6 in favor of a 200 horsepower V-8 or even a 210 horsepower supercharged V-6. Handling is well-balanced and predictable.

Anti-lock brakes are optional on the T-bird, air bags are not available and the car can be ordered with either a four-speed automatic or five-speed manual transmission.

## OLDSMOBILE EIGHTY EIGHT ROYALE
CATEGORY: Full-sized sedan
BASE PRICE: $18,495
ASSEMBLED IN: Wentzville, Mo.; Flint, Mich.

*1992 Oldsmobile Eighty Eight Royale SL*

*Auto Week* magazine recently tested an Olds Eighty Eight with traction control—a system that uses ABS sensors to stop tire slip on snow and ice—against foreign models similarly equipped. The surprising result was the Eighty-Eight often outperformed a traction-control-equipped BMW that cost thousands more.

But even without traction control, the Eighty Eight has a winning combination of crisp exterior styling, responsive handling and a healthy V-6 powerplant. There's plenty of room for five passengers, six in a pinch.

If the Olds has a shortcoming, it is the design of its instrument panel, which seems to have more tiny buttons and knobs than a small airplane. But that is a minor vice when compared to its considerable virtues.

## BUICK LE SABRE
CATEGORY: Full-sized sedan
BASE PRICE RANGE: $19,250-$21,330
ASSEMBLED IN: Flint, Mich.

*1992 Buick Le Sabre Limited*

The Le Sabre comes as close to being the all-American family car as one could hope. It has the same V-6 engine and interior room as its big brother, the Park Avenue, but it is five inches shorter and 200 pounds lighter. That makes for a better power to weight ratio.

The result is a car with smooth, reliable power, plenty of room for people and luggage, and a price that isn't too hard to take. A driver's air bag is standard, and anti-lock brakes are optional. One option worth considering is the Gran Touring Package, which includes a tauter suspension, larger tires and a gear ratio that favors better acceleration.

The previous version of the Le Sabre won high marks for quality in J.D. Power surveys and a large, loyal following in the car-buying public. Buick hopes the same will hold true for its newest Le Sabre, and early reviews seem encouraging.

## PONTIAC BONNEVILLE
CATEGORY: Sports sedan
BASE PRICE RANGE: $19,154-$28,600
ASSEMBLED IN: Wentzville, Mo.

*1992 Pontiac Bonneville SE with Sport Package*

No other car says more about the bold self-assurance of America's best auto designers than Pontiac's redesigned Bonneville. The lines of the Bonneville flow smoothly inside and out, yet no apparent compromises were made in the name of style.

In fact, this is one car in which every control and gauge seems to be perfectly placed and easy to see. Seating is roomy and comfortable, front and back, and the interior abounds in thoughtful amenities such as flip-out cup holders and parcel pass-throughs to the trunk.

Powered by a 170-horsepower version of GM's venerable 3.8-liter V-6, the Bonneville has the sweetest part of its power band where most American drivers need it—on the lower half of the speedometer.

All Bonnevilles feature a slick four-speed manual transmission and driver's side air bag. Options include traction control, passenger air bags and anti-lock brakes.

## BUICK ROADMASTER
CATEGORY: Extra-large full-sized car
BASE PRICE RANGE: $22,420-$24,750
ASSEMBLED IN: Arlington, Texas.; Willow Run, Mich.

*1992 Buick Roadmaster Limited*

This is what most people mean when they say "big car." *Car & Driver* noted in its *1992 Buyer's Guide* that the Roadmaster is so wide, a six-footer could lay transversely in the trunk. But why bother, when there's enough room for four on the back seat alone!

The Roadmaster is also the closest modern-day approximation of what people mean when they talk about a traditional American car. It is powered by a 5.7-liter V-8 engine, which kicks out 180 horsepower. Just the thing for cruising down the turnpike.

But it has some modern innovations that even die-hard traditionalists would be likely to appreciate, such as a standard driver's air bag and anti-lock brakes. And despite its size, it still manages to get 16 miles per gallon in the city, not bad for a car that weighs more than two tons.

## BUICK PARK AVENUE
CATEGORY: Full-sized luxury car
BASE PRICE RANGE: $25,885-$29,380
ASSEMBLED IN: Wentzville, Mo.

*1992 Buick Park Avenue*

Some cars are more than the sum of their parts. The Park Avenue is such a car. With exterior lines that evoke a Jaguar and a capacious interior that seats six with ease, the Park Avenue is blessed with good performance, fine road manners and a lot of handy features.

Not the least of these features are Park Avenue's available dual climate controls, built into each of the front doors, which allows driver and front seat passenger to avoid interior temperature arguments. The Park Avenue also features a smooth 3.8-liter V-6 mated to GM's wonderful four-speed automatic transmission. The "Ultra" version features a supercharger and generates 205 horsepower.

Despite a curb weight of more than 3,500 pounds, the Park Avenue still manages a respectable 18 miles per gallon in the city and 27 on the highway. That means the owner of this car can both have his large luxury cruiser and be a responsible consumer of fossil fuels at the same time.

## CADILLAC ELDORADO
CATEGORY: Luxury performance coupe
BASE PRICE: $33,377-$35,877
ASSEMBLED IN: Detroit, Mich.

*1992 Cadillac Eldorado*

Those who want some of the flair of the new Seville (see below) in a more Americanized coupe can find it in the new Eldorado, which is almost a foot longer than the model it replaces. Quiet and powerful in the great Cadillac tradition, it has a Zebrano wood-trimmed interior befitting a European luxury coupe.

The wallowy ride and handling characteristics of the old Cadillac boats is not in evidence here, especially if one opts for the Touring Coupe package. Besides a retuned suspension, the touring coupe also features a different color scheme and high performance tires.

In either configuration, the Eldorado, Cadillac hopes, will appeal to a younger set of drivers than its traditional customer base. We think they will succeed, although the exterior styling lacks the cohesiveness of the spectacular Seville.

## LINCOLN CONTINENTAL
CATEGORY: Luxury sedan
BASIC PRICE RANGE: $33, 138-$35, 327
ASSEMBLED IN: Wixom, Mich.

*1992 Lincoln Continental*

Some cars flaunt their virtues. Others express them in subtle ways. The Lincoln Continental belongs to the second group. Redesigned several years ago, this big Lincoln gets smoother and more solid, in look and feel, year after year.

The power before the driver's throne is a front-drive V-6 with 155 horsepower, a 15-horse improvement over the year before. More impressive is a sytem of electronically activated shock absorbers and air springs that give the Continental impressive poise in corners or over rough pavement.

The lucky occupants are buttressed from a hostile world by leather-covered seats, a battery of power accessories and a generally commendable stereo system. But in the worst of circumstances, it is also comforting to know they have the protection of standard anti-lock brakes and standard air bags for driver and passenger.

## CHEVROLET CORVETTE
CATEGORY: Sports car
BASE PRICE RANGE: $34,604-$69,455
ASSEMBLED IN: Bowling Green, Ky.

*1992 Chevrolet Corvette*

Just because this Corvette looks like Corvettes have looked for so many years doesn't mean this is the same old 'Vette. The Corvette has been improved in so many ways for 1992 that it will make your head snap.

So, too, will its acceleration. This year's 'Vette has a 300 horsepower base engine. More important are dozens of refinements, large and small, that have eliminated body squeaks, enhanced instrument readability, upgraded component durability and improved handling—through a thoroughly revised suspension system.

The most surprising feature of all about this year's Corvette, however, may be that, in addition to having standard anti-lock brakes, the two-seater now sports standard traction control. Traction control prevents unintended wheel slip on ice or snow. That makes this year's Corvette, though a rear-wheel-drive sports car, a surprisingly easy car to drive all year. That way, the fun never stops.

## CADILLAC SEVILLE
CATEGORY: Luxury sports sedan
BASE PRICE RANGE: $36,133- $39,433
ASSEMBLED IN: Detroit, Mich.

*1992 Cadillac Seville Touring Sedan*

This car has been chosen by *Motor Trend* as its car of the year and is on the Ten Best lists of every other top automotive magazine in the country. Little wonder.

The Seville, particularly in STS trim, can compete head to head with Lexus and Infiniti. Its low-slung, purposeful body telegraphs the joys that lie within both the cockpit and the engine compartment. The Seville's interior is a symphony of leather and wood, evocative of an expensive Audi. The seats are supportive, the instrumentation is well-placed and easy to read, and every control falls readily to hand.

The engine, a 4.9-liter V-8, cranks out a respectable 200 horsepower, while the fully independent suspension and standard anti-lock brakes make sure you are able to deal with all that power. The fact that customers have been on waiting lists to buy this car from dealerships in domestic-car-phobic Los Angeles says a lot about its appeal even to well-heeled import devotees.

## DODGE VIPER
CATEGORY: Raw sports car
BASE PRICE (EST.): $55,000
ASSEMBLED IN: Detroit, Mich.

*1992 Dodge Viper RT/10*

There is nothing rational about this car. Nobody needs a two-seat roadster without real windows or outside door handles. Nobody needs a 400 horsepower V-10 aluminum block engine that can reach 60 miles an hour from a standing start in less than five seconds.

Nobody needs a pair of side exhaust pipes that, if you aren't careful, can burn your legs as you leave the car after a bout of spirited driving.

Sure, nobody needs the Viper. But many people want one. And once you've seen one crouching, low, mean and wide in a parking lot, or if you get to drive this remarkable car, you may want one, too. The Viper is a sheet-metal embodiment of American car passion.

## PLYMOUTH GRAND VOYAGER /DODGE GRAND CARAVAN
CATEGORY: Minivan
BASE PRICE: $17,281
ASSEMBLED IN: St. Louis, Mo.

*1992 Plymouth Grand Voyager LE*

No matter how hard they try, nobody—not the Japanese manufacturers, not General Motors, not Ford—can make a better minivan than Chrysler, the company that invented the minivan more than a decade ago.

The latest iterations of the Caravan and Voyager only help to prove that point. Redesigned in 1991, the twins continue to dazzle their loyal buyers with performance and utility features the rivals can't match. But now it's all wrapped up in a lovely interior with sweep-around styling.

For 1992, these models, which featured the first driver's-side air bags, in a minivan, also have optional integrated kiddie seats which can be tucked away when adults are riding. Neat, huh? But if your priorities are a car assembled in the United States, be sure to consider only the "Grand" models of Voyager and Caravan built in St. Louis; all other Voyager and Caravan models are assembled in Canada.

FORD EXPLORER
CATEGORY: Sport utility vehicle
BASE PRICE RANGE: $16,339-$24,038
ASSEMBLED IN: Louisville, Ky.

*1992 Ford Explorer*

Just how good is the Ford Explorer? So good that Mazda chose to rebadge a two-door version of the Explorer as the Mazda Navajo rather than design and build its own model. It's so good and its sales so strong that it has never been rebated in the two years since its introduction.

What makes the Explorer such a paragon of all-purpose virtue? Just about everything. Its ride and handling are remarkably smooth—either on or off the road. It is big enough inside to accommodate four passengers with ease, six in a pinch, with plenty of room left over for luggage.

In addition, its 160 horsepower V-6 gets the Explorer going in a hurry, while its standard anti-lock braking system helps it to stop in a hurry.

## JEEP GRAND CHEROKEE
CATEGORY: sport utility vehicle
BASE PRICE (EST.) $24,000
ASSEMBLED IN: Detroit, Mich.

*1993 Jeep Grand Cherokee Limited*

As good as the Ford Explorer may be, some think the 1993 Grand Cherokee might be even better. It took Jeep designers and engineers six years to cook up this new model, which is 7.7 inches longer and a bit wider inside than its predecessor.

Propelled by a 190 horsepower V-6, the suspension has been tuned so well that those who have tested it say it feels almost as good off the road as on it.

You also are given a choice of three different four-wheel-drive systems. "We are mightily impressed," said *Automobile* magazine in a recent review. Maybe you will be, too.

## OLDS BRAVADA
CATEGORY: Sport utility vehicle
BASE PRICE: $25,070
ASSEMBLED IN: Moraine, Ohio

*1992 Oldsmobile Bravada*

The words "luxury" and "truck" rarely belong in the same sentence—unless you are talking about the Oldsmobile Bravada, an all-purpose vehicle with real upscale appeal.

While the Bravada uses the same chassis as the GMC Jimmy four-door, it enjoys significant enhancements. The Bravada has standard anti-lock brakes and a wonderful full-time four-wheel-drive system, for openers, which can help it stop and go almost anywhere without much effort.

The interior of the Bravada, with its four doors and four seats, is done up with a sort of opulence that may make you think twice about driving it with your work boots on. Once you stick your boot to the accelerator, however, you'll know you're piloting a heavy-duty machine, particularly if you opt for the 200 horsepower V-6 engine.

## FORD F-SERIES
CATEGORY: Pickup truck
BASE PRICE RANGE: $10,921-$21,603
ASSEMBLED IN: Kansas City, Mo.

*A 1992 Ford F-Series pickup truck*

Contrary to what you may have heard, the best selling vehicle in the United States is not the Honda Accord. For several years now, it has been the F-Series truck. Part of the secret may be variety. After all, you can order your F-series truck in 30 different combinations.

This year the F-10 line includes a stepside bed model and will be restyled in front with new headlights.

When *Automobile* magazine tested an F-150 XLT Lariat, the reviewer fairly gushed. "All inconveniences–potholes, curbs, Hyundais—become small and trivial," he wrote. "...driving an F-150 gives an unmistakable sense of privilege, and that's good."

But be aware that not all F-series trucks are built in the United States. Some are assembled in Canada. Be sure to check.

## CHEVROLET S-10 PICKUP
CATEGORY: Pickup truck
BASE PRICE RANGE: $9,192- $15,394
ASSEMBLED IN: Moraine, Ohio; Pontiac, Mich.;
Shreveport, La.

*1992 Chevrolet S-10 2WD long box pickup*

Although times have been tough for domestic manufacturers in the far West, this truck line has done surprisingly well in Los Angeles, of all places, where young people have been buying them like hot cakes.

The reasons? The S-10 prices begin at $9,000, making it cheap, and in the hands of creative young owners the truck seems to lend itself to wild color schemes, which have never stopped being popular in La La Land.

That shouldn't lead you to believe this is a truck for showing off instead of working. There are enough options in terms of engines and payload capacities to handle anything from the boulevard to the brick yard. And if you want to spend more money on this model, there are plenty of ways to do it, by specifying power windows or locks, air conditioning, tilt steering wheel, and a high-end stereo.

# Transplants

There are, of course, Japanese companies assembling cars in the U.S. These so-called "transplants" do provide American assembly jobs and contain significantly more U.S. content than what the University of Michigan Transportation Center estimates to be an average of only 1 percent U.S. content of cars built in Japan.

However, the profits from the sale of these transplants go back to Japan, and the design and engineering generally takes place in Japan–not the U.S. These cars also contain much less U.S. content than their American counterparts assembled in the U.S. Consequently, it is still more helpful to the U.S. economy to avoid these transplants and buy an American nameplate car assembled in the U.S.

But if you feel you just have to buy a car with a Japanese nameplate, be sure to give your strongest consideration to one of the following models, all of which are assembled in the United States.

To give you an idea of the relative good purchasing one of these cars will do the U.S. economy, we have included a rating from the Detroit Free Press Index of American Content for each model. This index considers the relative value of each of the four factors discussed above—nameplate, design and engineering, content and assembly—and then assigns the model an index number from one to 100 with 100 being the most American and 1 the least. For comparison purposes, consumers should note that most U.S. nameplate cars evaluated by this same index scored at least 65, with a great many scoring between 78 and 100.

**FORD PROBE/MAZDA MX-6**
CATEGORY: Sports coupes
BASE PRICE RANGE: $12,587-$17,255
ASSEMBLED IN: Flat Rock, Mich.
COMPANY ASSEMBLING: Mazda
DETROIT FREE PRESS INDEX: Probe 78, MX-6 46

The Ford Probe and Mazda MX-6 are both sporty coupes built at a Mazda plant in Flat Rock, Mich., and while they share Mazda engines and drivetrains, they are very different in the looks department.

The newest MX-6 carries on a Japanese obsession with refinement. It shares the gumdrop looks of myriad cars that all seem to be descended in one form or another from a randy Ford Taurus. The interior and exterior styling, while in no way offensive, can hardly be called exciting.

In contrast, though it is a Ford-designed product, the Probe looks distinctly unlike the rest of its bloodline. It features an aggressive, snout-like nose, flip-up headlamps, and smooth, almost futuristic lines. It has become surprisingly popular in Europe, particularly Germany.

Both cars will be extensively restyled in 1993 and will be available in 1993 with 24-valve V-6 natural power instead of the turbocharged inline four that was top engine in previous models.

## PLYMOUTH LASER/ EAGLE TALON/ MITSUBISHI ECLIPSE
CATEGORY: Sports coupes
BASE PRICE RANGE: $11,552-$20,017
ASSEMBLED IN: Normal, Ill.
COMPANY ASSEMBLING: Mitsubishi-owned Diamond Star Motors
DETROIT FREE PRESS INDEX: 68 (Plymouth Laser)

These sporty cars seat two with ease, four in a pinch, but can go and stop with gusto. The five-speed gearbox mated to the turbocharged engine can make for a howling good time.

The sleek exteriors of these cars contrast a bit with the interiors, which feature oddly canted ventilation louvers that may make you wonder if your car was used in side-impact collision tests. But thoughtful touches and a first-class stereo system make up for such eccentricities. Outfitted with optional all-wheel-drive, these cars become particularly fun to drive in the snow and rain. But in any configuration, these cars, though mostly designed in Japan and filled with Japanese parts, are the pride of Normal, Ill.

### HONDA ACCORD
CATEGORY: Family sedan, coupe and wagon
BASE PRICE RANGE: $13,515-$19,285
ASSEMBLED IN: Marysville, Ohio; East Liberty, Ohio
COMPANY ASSEMBLING: Honda of America
DETROIT FREE PRESS INDEX: 46

If the best selling car in America has to have a Japanese nameplate, at least it is assembled in the United States—in addition to being a very good car.

The Honda Accord has a lot going for it. It is well-built, performs like a champ, delivers reasonable fuel economy and has plenty of room for the family and a large load of luggage. At last, the Accord can be ordered with air bags and anti-lock brakes, making it a safer bet in an accident as well.

To Honda's credit, too, the company has made a commendable effort for a Japanese corporation to move even more of the design and assembly process to the United States. Now, for example, the engines in many Honda products are cast and assembled along with the cars themselves—in and near Marysville, Ohio. And much of the design work on the coupe and station wagon versions was done in this country.

### HONDA CIVIC SEDAN
CATEGORY: Economy sedan
BASE PRICE RANGE: $9,900-$14,615
ASSEMBLED IN: Marysville, Ohio
COMPANY ASSEMBLING: Honda of America
DETROIT FREE PRESS INDEX: 46

Once upon a time, the Civic was a tiny car but a great big value, both in price and fuel economy. As the years have gone by, however, the Civic has grown in size and has shrunk in fuel economy. Today, it is about as big as one of the Accords of yore. And its price has bumped it out of the "econobox" category.

Nevertheless, the car still makes reviewers marvel with its fine road manners and high quality construction. In fact, *Car and Driver* called the new Civic a luxury car that has been left in the dryer too long.

The Civic can be had with several optional four-cylinder engines, ranging from a 70 horsepower model to one that cranks out 102 horsepower. Anti-lock brakes are an option and a driver's side air bag is standard. Like its big brother, the Accord, the Civic sedan is assembled in Marysville, Ohio, though other body configurations are imported from Japan.

### NISSAN SENTRA
CATEGORY: Economy sedan, coupe
BASE PRICE RANGE: $8,795-$13,975
ASSEMBLED IN: Smyrna, Tenn.
COMPANY ASSEMBLING: Nissan
DETROIT FREE PRESS INDEX: 46

Those who know the older model of Sentra know it as a sharply angular and somewhat spartan car. But the newest Sentra, built in Smyrna, Tenn., stands in smooth contrast.

Sleeker inside and out, the Sentra features a 110 horse-power, 1.6-liter base engine that is more than adequate to its task. But 140 horsepower turns this meek hauler into a much more aggressive little package.

In fact *Car and Driver* named the Sentra SE-R to its list of the 10 best cars of 1992. And more than one reviewer has compared it to the old BMW 2002 as a thrifty way to have first-class driving fun.

### TOYOTA CAMRY
CATEGORY: Full-sized sedan
BASE PRICE RANGE: $17,103-$20,803
ASSEMBLED IN: Georgetown, Ky.
COMPANY ASSEMBLING: Toyota

DETROIT FREE PRESS INDEX :   Toyota chose not to respond to the Detroit Free Press survey.

Few Japanese nameplate cars have won as many kudos over the years as the Camry, and the latest model carries on the tradition. The newest model Camry, assembled in Kentucky, handles and performs with great elan while it has plenty of room for a family.

It has all the natty interior appointments and sense of exterior bulk and presence worthy of models costing thousands more, especially the smallest model Lexus sedan, the ES 300, with which it shares its chassis.

Little wonder the Camry with the V-6 engine was chosen one of *Car and Driver's* 10 best cars of 1991.

# Index

## Made in the USA™
### Foundation

**Put America Back To Work**

**Stop Foreign Corporations From Ripping Off American Taxpayers**

**Make Sure We Leave A Strong America For Our Children And Grandchildren**

# *Join The Made In The USA Foundation*

For more information, fill out and return postcard

Name _____

Address _____

City _____ State _____ Zip Code _____

Telephone _____

**Made in the USA** ™
**Foundation**

**MADE IN THE USA FOUNDATION**
1800 Diagonal Road
Suite 180
Alexandria, VA 22314